Patterns of Inequality in the Indian Labour Market, 1983-2012

Published by
ACADEMIC FOUNDATION
in association with

INSTITUTE FOR HUMAN DEVELOPMENT

CEBRAP
centro brasileiro de análise e planejamento

ABOUT THE AUTHORS:

Gerry Rodgers is presently Visiting Professor at the Institute for Human Development (IHD), New Delhi. He holds an M.A. (Cambridge University) and D.Phil (Sussex University) in Economic Development. For over 30 years he worked at the International Labour Office (ILO) in a variety of positions, including Director of the International Institute for Labour Studies. His work has mainly been concerned with poverty, inequality, labour, human resources and employment, especially in India, Southeast Asia and Latin America, and he has published widely in these fields. He was also the principal author of a book on the history of the ILO. His recent research has been on inclusive development in Bihar, where he has been undertaking studies for over 40 years, and on the differing experiences of labour market inequality in Brazil and India.

Vidhya Soundararajan is an applied micro economist who focuses on development and labour economics. Her work examines the impact of labour market institutions and regulations on employment, wages, productivity, and inequality in low wage labour markets. She is a senior research associate at the IHD, Delhi, and a PhD candidate in Applied Economics at Cornell University. Prior to this, she worked at the World Bank, International Food Policy Research Institute, and the Planning Commission of India, where her work centred on agricultural value chains and rural development programmes in India. She holds an M.S. degree in Economics from Madras School of Economics, and a B.Tech degree in Information Technology from Anna University.

Patterns of Inequality in the Indian Labour Market, 1983-2012

GERRY RODGERS
VIDHYA SOUNDARARAJAN

INSTITUTE FOR HUMAN DEVELOPMENT
NEW DELHI

www.ihdindia.org

ACADEMIC FOUNDATION
NEW DELHI

www.academicfoundation.org

First published in 2016
by

ACADEMIC FOUNDATION
4772-73 / 23 Bharat Ram Road, (23 Ansari Road),
Darya Ganj, New Delhi - 110 002 (India).
Phones : 23245001 / 02 / 03 / 04.
Fax : +91-11-23245005.
E-mail : books@academicfoundation.com
www.academicfoundation.org

in association with the
Institute for Human Development, New Delhi.

Disclaimer:
The findings/views/opinions expressed in this book are solely those of the authors and do not necessarily reflect the views of the publisher.

Cataloging in Publication Data--DK
Courtesy: D.K. Agencies (P) Ltd. <docinfo@dkagencies.com>

Rodgers, Gerry, author.
Patterns of inequality in the Indian labour market, 1983-2012 / Gerry Rodgers, Vidhya Soundararajan.
pages cm
Includes bibliographical references.
ISBN 9789332703575

1. Labor market--India--History. 2. Income distribution--India--History. I. Soundararajan, Vidhya, author. II. Institute for Human Development (New Delhi, India), issuing body. III. Title.

HD5819.R63 2016 DDC 331.120954 23

Typeset, printed and bound by The Book Mint, New Delhi.
www.thebookmint.in

CONTENTS

List of Tables and Figures

TABLES

FIGURES

Preface

This monograph was prepared as part of a research project on labour market inequality in Brazil and India, carried out by the Brazilian Centre for Analysis and Planning (Cebrap), São Paulo and the Institute for Human Development (IHD), New Delhi, with support from the Canadian International Development Research Centre (IDRC).

High inequality in income and welfare is a major policy concern in both Brazil and India. Over the last decade, the connections between inequality and growth, and between inequality and poverty reduction, have been receiving increasing attention in both national and international development communities. There are many sources of income inequality—production structures, the distribution of assets, the relative power of capital and labour, political forces and social hierarchy, as well as differences in education and capability. But among these many factors, labour market structures and institutions are of central importance. Understanding the pattern of labour market inequality and its determinants is therefore essential.

The Cebrap-IHD research project addresses these issues and their implications for development policies in both Brazil and India. The trends in inequality in the two countries are different, and it is important to understand why, how far this results from underlying social and economic institutions and relationships, and how far from policy choices and their implementation. The project aims to add to knowledge and contribute to policy choice through in-depth comparisons of the relationships and outcomes in the two countries. More details are available at *www.ihdindia.org/lmi*

The present monograph presents quantitative evidence on the dimensions and trends in inequality in India since the 1980s. It was prepared in parallel with similar research in Brazil, and other papers compare the outcomes in the two countries (in particular Cacciamali et al., 2015 and Barbosa et al., forthcoming).

This monograph has greatly benefitted from the contributions and comments of the other members of the project teams in the two countries, in particular Nandita Gupta, Taniya Chakrabarty and Janine Rodgers from the IHD and Maria-Cristina Cacciamali, Fabio Tatei, Ian Prates and Alexandre de Freitas Barbosa from Cebrap. Sandip Sarkar of IHD read and gave helpful comments on an earlier draft.

We are grateful to Alakh N. Sharma, Director of IHD, for hosting this project, contributing to its development and helping in its work. Jayati Ghosh and the late T.S. Papola gave a great deal of valuable advice. We are also grateful to Edgard Rodriguez of IDRC for his unfailing support.

—Gerry Rodgers and Vidhya Soundararajan
March 2016, New Delhi.

Introduction

This monograph provides a quantitative picture of some of the most important correlates of inequality in wages and expenditure in India. It does not stand on its own, but is designed as a complement to a second publication, currently under preparation, entitled: *Growth, Labour and Inequality in Brazil and India: A Comparative Study*, which sets the analysis of inequality in a broader context, draws on similar work in Brazil, and discusses the literature on many of the relationships examined here (Barbosa et al., forthcoming). For that reason there is little review of or reference to the existing literature in this monograph.

The main data source is the National Sample Survey (NSS). Four rounds of the survey have been used for the paper: 1983 (38th round), 1993-94 (50th round), 2004-05 (61st round) and 2011-12 (68th round), covering both employment and consumer expenditure. These four years provide a good picture of long term trends. All were average or fairly good agricultural years, which helps to moderate the effects of fluctuations in agricultural production on wages and incomes. They also cover the periods both before and after the economic reforms of the early 1990s.

Other data sources used include the National Council of Applied Economic Research (NCAER) Human Development Survey for 2004-05. This, like the NSS, is a national household survey, which covers some additional topics, notably household income. It therefore permits us to compare income inequality with inequality of wages and expenditure. The monograph also uses some data from the Annual Survey of Industry (ASI) and from National Accounts, as well as price indices compiled by the Ministry of Labour. For more details on data sources see *Data Sources for the Analysis of Labour Market*

Inequality in Brazil and India by Alexandre de Freitas Barbosa, Maria Cristina Cacciamali, Gerry Rodgers, Vidhya Soundararajan, Fabio Tatei, Rogerio Barbosa, J. Krishnamurty.[1]

The two principal dimensions of inequality in the labour market concern inequality in labour incomes, and inequality in access to employment. This monograph mainly examines labour incomes, though we also consider some aspects of unequal access to employment. The NSS provides data on the wages of all employed household members, but not on income from self-employment. In practice, then, we focus on wage inequality. The NSS also collects information on household expenditure. Expenditure can be used as a proxy for overall income, including not only all sources of labour income but also income from interest, rent and other sources. However, labour income is by far the largest component of income, except in the highest income groups.

Chapter 1 gives broad trends in patterns of inequality of wages and of expenditure. Chapter 2 then decomposes wage inequality in terms of five principal factors: type of work, gender, social group, education and region. Chapter 3 presents a similar, though more limited exercise for household expenditure. Chapter 4 brings these variables together in a multivariate decomposition of inequality. Chapter 5 gives some comparisons between measures of inequality in wages, expenditure and income. Chapter 6 examines the macro-level question of the functional distribution of income. Chapter 7 considers some aspects of unequal access to different occupations, and the wage differentials between them. Finally, Chapter 8 concludes.

1. IHD Working Paper 03/2014.

1

Trends in Inequality

1.1 Wages

Basic data on wages and wage inequality are given in Figures 1.1 to 1.9 (for India as a whole, and separately for rural and urban areas). Sources for these figures and, except where otherwise indicated, for other figures and tables in this monograph are unit level data from the National Sample Survey Organisation (NSSO) employment and unemployment and household expenditure surveys for 1983, 1993-94, 2004-05 and 2011-12.

Figure 1.1

Mean Real Wages: All India (₹/Day at 2004-05 Prices)

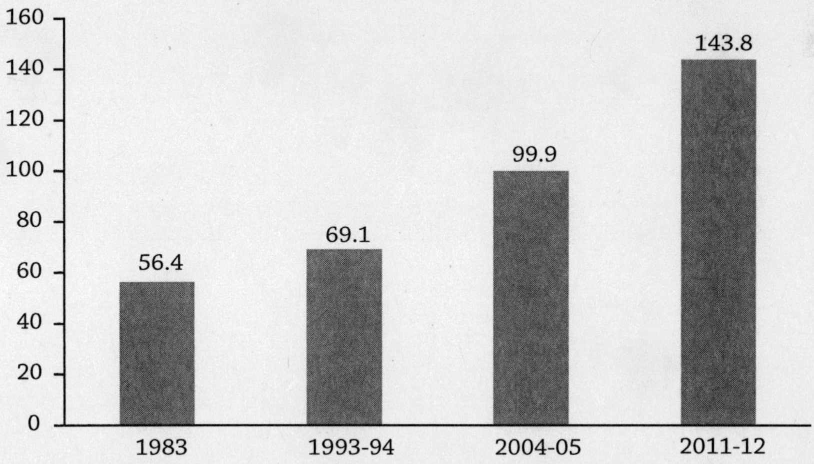

Note: In all figures 1983 refers to calendar year 1983, 1994 to the year July 1993 to June 1994, 2005 to the year July 2004 to June 2005 and 2012 to the year July 2011 to June 2012. These are the field work periods for the surveys concerned.

Figure 1.1 shows the trend in real wages over time. Money wages were converted to 2004-05 prices using the consumer price series for industrial workers in urban areas, and for agricultural labourers in rural areas (Table 1.1).

Table 1.1

Price Indices for Industrial Workers and Agricultural Labourers

	CPI-IW (Base 1982=100)	*Standardised CPI-IW*	*CPI-AL (Base 1986-87=100)*	*Standardised CPI-AL*
1983	102.2	0.20	85.4	0.25
1993-1994	257.9	0.50	203.8	0.60
2004-2005	519.5	1.00	339.5	1.00
2011-2012	891.8	1.72	613.7	1.81

Notes: CPI-IW is the consumer price index for industrial workers; CPI-AL is the consumer price index for agricultural labour.
Source: Indian Labour Bureau (*labourbureau.nic.in*).

Overall, mean wages grew throughout this period at an accelerating pace, 1.9 per cent per year between 1983 and 1993-94, 3.4 per cent per year between 1993-94 and 2004-05 and 5.3 per cent between 2004-05 and 2011-12. Clearly wage workers shared in the growth of the Indian economy. On the other hand, the growth of wages was lower than the growth of GDP (gross domestic product) per capita (2.7%, 4.4% and 6.9% per annum in the three periods concerned). One implication of this difference in growth rates is that wage income declined relative to income from capital and other sources, and that this gap was increasing over time. We examine the functional distribution of income in more detail in Chapter 6.

Both rural and urban areas shared in this growth in wages. Over the period as a whole, rural wages rose by 3.5 per cent per year; urban wages by 2.9 per cent. The rural to urban wage ratio rose from 0.36 in 1983 to 0.43 in 2011-12. We can therefore conclude that rural-urban inequality in the labour market declined at the aggregate level.

This shift in favour of rural wages was greater in the more recent period. Rural wages grew by 2.3 per cent from 1983 to 1993-94, compared with 2.2 for urban. From 1993-94 to 2004-05 rural wages grew at 3.6 per cent and urban at 2.2; from 2004-05 to 2011 rural wages grew at 5.2 per cent and urban at 4.7 per cent.

There are a variety of different ways to characterise wage inequality. Figures 1.2 and 1.3 give the most common overall measures, the Theil index[1] and the Gini coefficient. The Gini coefficient is the most widespread single measure, but the Theil index has the advantage that it can easily be decomposed into inequality within and between particular groups, a property which we use in later Chapters.

Figure 1.2

Theil Index for Wages: All India

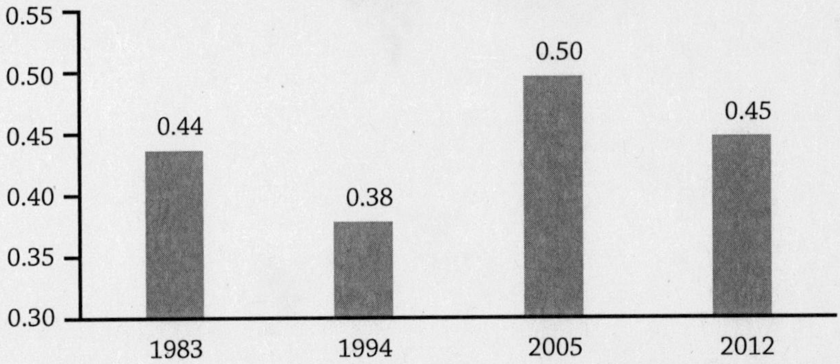

Figure 1.3

Gini Index for Wages: All India

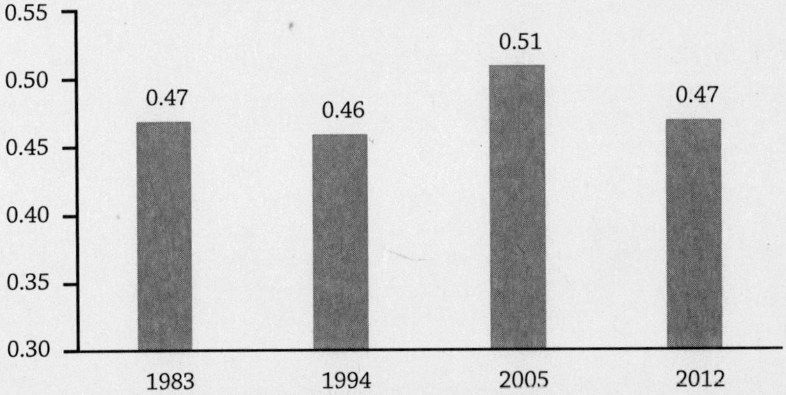

1. We use the Theil t index [GE (1)] throughout.

The Theil index for wage inequality overall shows a clear pattern over time (Figure 1.2). Inequality fell between 1983 and 1993-94, rose between 1993-94 and 2004-05, and fell again between 2004-05 and 2011-12. The overall level of the index at the end of the period was not much different from its level at the beginning. The Gini index shows a similar pattern (Figure 1.3), except that the reduction in inequality in the 1980s was less, and the rise after 1993-94 was greater.

A rural-urban breakdown suggests that this overall picture was the result of opposite trends in rural and urban areas (Figures 1.4 and 1.5). In rural areas, the Theil index declined overall, with a reversal between 1993-94 and 2004-05. This pattern has some similarity with the overall trend, except that the reversal in the middle period was offset by an equally large decline between 2004-05 and 2011-12. In urban areas, however, wage inequality rose sharply in period 2, but instead of declining thereafter continued to rise to some extent in period 3. Once again, the Gini coefficient shows a very similar pattern.[2]

Both Theil and Gini indices reduce a complex pattern of inequality to a single figure, and it is also interesting to look at specific aspects of the distribution. Figures 1.6 to 1.8 give the 10:10 ratio, that is to say the ratio between the average wage of the top 10 per cent and the bottom 10 per cent of the wage distribution. It is therefore a measure of how far the distribution is stretched at the extremes. Overall, we find that the ratio between the top and the bottom for the population as a whole narrowed in period 1, from 17.6 to 16.6. It then increased considerably in period 2, from 16.6 to 20.2, before falling back to 16.2 in period 3 (Figure 1.6). This pattern is similar to that of the Gini and Theil coefficients for the period as a whole.

2. We will use 'period 1' for 1983 to 1993-94, 'period 2' for 1993-94 to 2004-05 and 'period 3' for 2004-05 to 2011-12.

Figure 1.4

Theil Index for Rural and Urban Wages

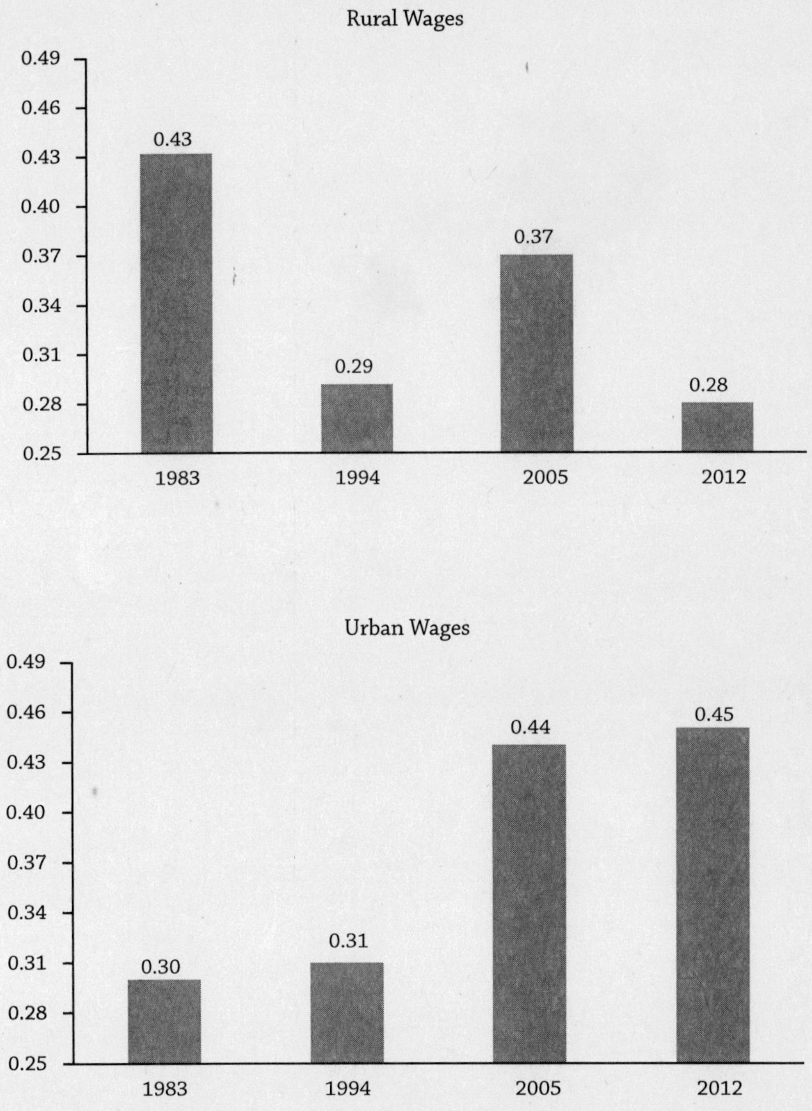

Figure 1.5

Gini Index for Rural and Urban Wages

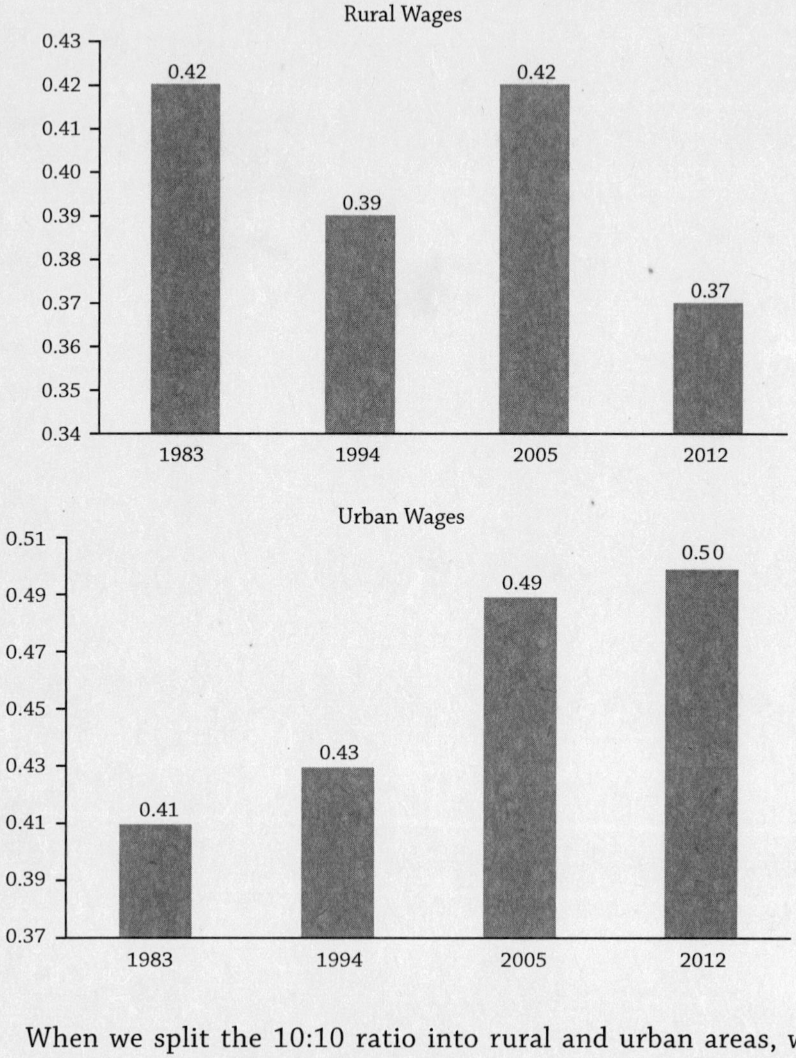

When we split the 10:10 ratio into rural and urban areas, we find some similarities and some differences with the Gini and Theil patterns. Overall we see that the 10:10 wage ratio is much higher in urban than in rural areas, which is as expected and consistent with the Gini and Theil results. In rural areas, the ratio fell in period 1, rose in period 2 and then fell again in period 3, so the overall trend was downwards, much like both Theil and Gini coefficients. In urban areas the trend was upwards in both periods 1 and 2, but there was some reversal after 2004-05, and the ratio fell back to its 1994 levels by 2011-12, although it remained significantly higher than in 1983. If we compare this with the Gini/Theil pattern, we see that the gap between the top and the bottom in urban areas was already widening before the economic reforms of the early 1990s, but this must have been compensated by some redistribution further down the income scale, since the Gini and Theil increased only slightly. In period 2 inequality rose for both measures, but the decline in the 10:10 ratio after 2004-05 differs from the Gini and Theil, which rose slightly. This suggests that the main gains were concentrated in upper wage earners below the top 10 per cent, or that the lowest wage earners did better than those just above them.

Figure 1.6

10:10 Wage Ratio, All India

(Ratio of Average Wages in Top Decile to Bottom Decile)

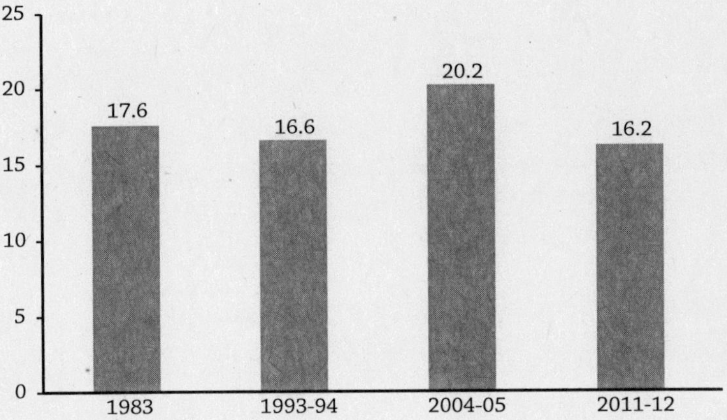

The distribution of wage income for workers at different levels of the wage distribution is presented in Figure 1.9. The share of the top 10 per cent of wage earners rose from 36 to 40 per cent over the period as a whole, and that of the middle 40 and bottom 50 fell, but most of the change occurred between 1993-94 and 2004-05. Overall, considering that this was a 30 year period with quite dramatic economic changes, it might well be concluded that the distribution of wage income was surprisingly stable, with some limited transfers from the middle and the bottom to the top.

Figure 1.7

10:10 Wage Ratio, Rural

(Ratio of Average Wages in Top Decile to Bottom Decile)

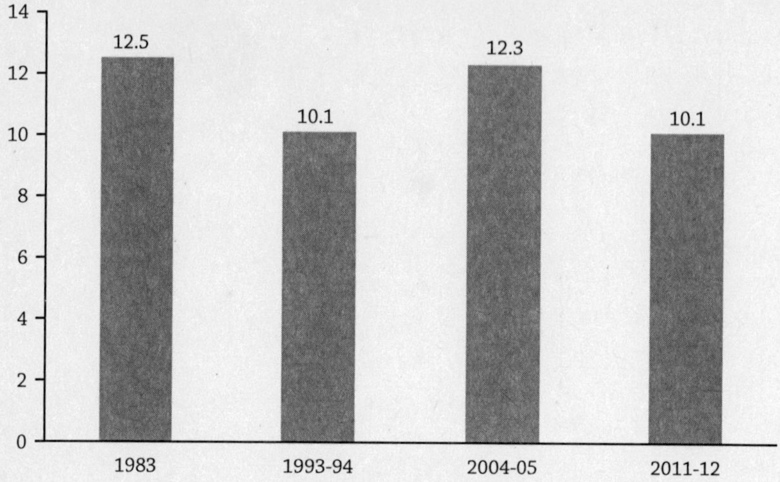

Figure 1.8

10:10 Wage Ratio, Urban

(Ratio of Average Wages in Top Decile to Bottom Decile)

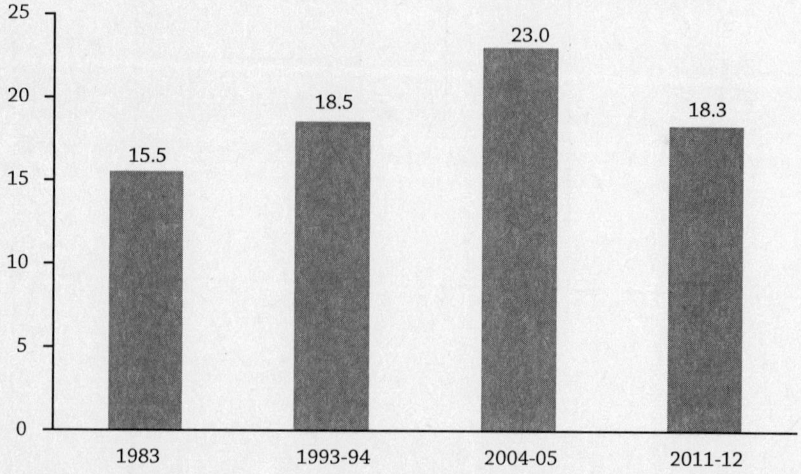

Figure 1.9

Overall Pattern of Distribution of Wage Income (All India)

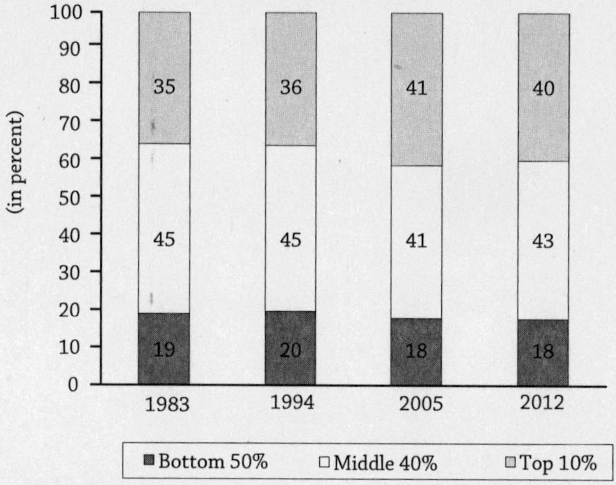

These different measures do not all tell exactly the same story, but there is a fairly consistent picture. On balance, inequality has increased since 1983 with the increase concentrated in urban areas and in the period 1994 to 2005; thereafter the tendency was for inequality to stabilise or decline, especially in rural areas, and helped by a reduction in the urban-rural wage gap. An increase in the share of the top 10 per cent was mainly at the expense of those in the middle of the distribution, rather than those at the bottom.

1.2 Expenditure Per Capita

Figure 1.10 shows that household expenditure per capita (using the National Sample Survey expenditure surveys[3]) rose at an annual rate of 1.7 per cent per annum in rural areas for the period as a whole, and slightly faster, 1.85 per cent in urban areas. The gap between rural and urban areas in expenditure is therefore widening slowly, although both are rising. This is the opposite of what was found for wages, where the gap between rural and urban areas was narrowing.

3. Expenditure data are also collected in the employment survey, but the data from the specialised expenditure survey carried out in the same rounds appear to be more reliable, so that source is used for this Chapter.

This is possible, because expenditure reflects self-employed incomes as well as wages. It would imply that self-employed incomes in rural areas were rising slower than wages or slower than self-employed incomes in urban areas. This is quite plausible if farm incomes were declining relative to wage incomes.

Figure 1.10

Real Monthly Household Expenditure Per Capita, Rural and Urban India (₹ at 2004-05 Prices)

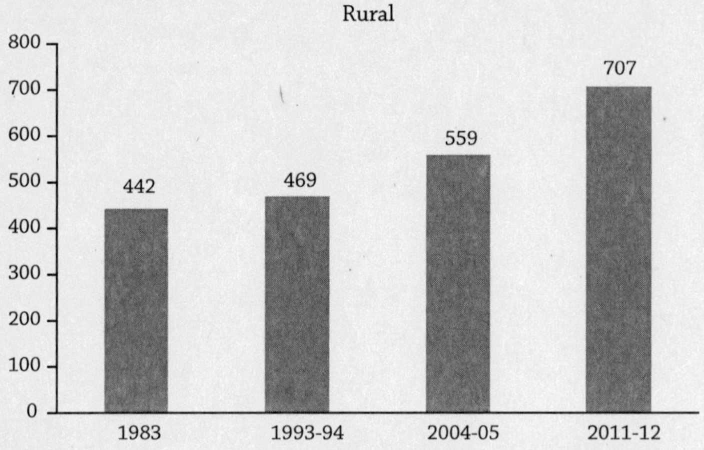

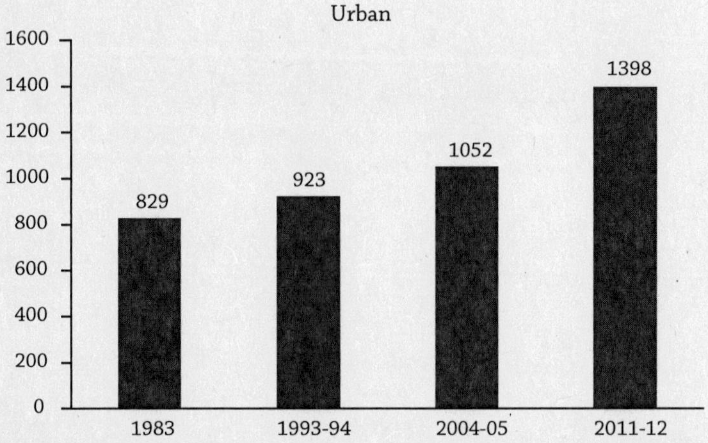

The growth in expenditure accelerated over time, 0.6 per cent per year in rural areas in period 1 against 1.0 per cent in urban areas; 1.6 against 1.2 in period 2; and 3.4 against 4.1 in period 3. These increases are notably 1.0 to 2.0 per cent less than the annual increases in real wages.

The general, systematic tendency is for the expenditure data to show lower inequality, whether measured by Theil or Gini, than the wage data. There are a number of reasons why a divergence is to be expected. One is a general tendency for expenditure to be less unequally distributed than income, which we discuss in Chapter 5. Another is that non-wage income (which of course affects expenditure) is likely to be less equally distributed than wage income. A third is that households will tend to have both male and female members, and often both young and old members, so wage inequality between these categories of workers is less reflected in aggregate household income.

The measures of expenditure inequality show little change between 1983 and 1993-94 overall, but this is the result of a decline in inequality within rural areas and an increase in urban areas (together with some increase in the gap between them) (Figures 1.11 to 1.13). This is quite consistent with the wage data, which also show some decline in inequality between these two dates in rural areas, and some increase in urban areas. However the wage data suggest that there was some decline in inequality overall, which is not the case for the expenditure data.

After 1993-94 and up to 2004-05, expenditure and wage measures coincide in showing a rather significant increase in inequality in both rural and urban areas, and overall. After 2004-05, however, the expenditure data diverge from the wage data, in rural areas at least, because overall expenditure inequality continues to rise, as measured by both Theil and Gini coefficients in both rural and urban areas, while in the wage data inequality fell in rural areas.

It is quite likely that this pattern reflects the growing integration of rural and urban areas. Rural households are increasingly gaining access to urban employment. This may have a different effect on wages and on expenditure. On wages, it may drive casual wages up in rural areas, because of the availability of higher-paying urban alternatives, and therefore reduce wage inequality. But at the same time, well-off rural households may have increasing access to incomes from urban areas, and indeed greater opportunities to spend this income. It is possible that trends in non-wage incomes also play a role. On this we have no direct information, but there is reason to believe that income from capital is increasing compared with wages, and this would tend to increase income inequality.

Figure 1.11

Theil and Gini Index of Household Expenditure Per Capita, All India

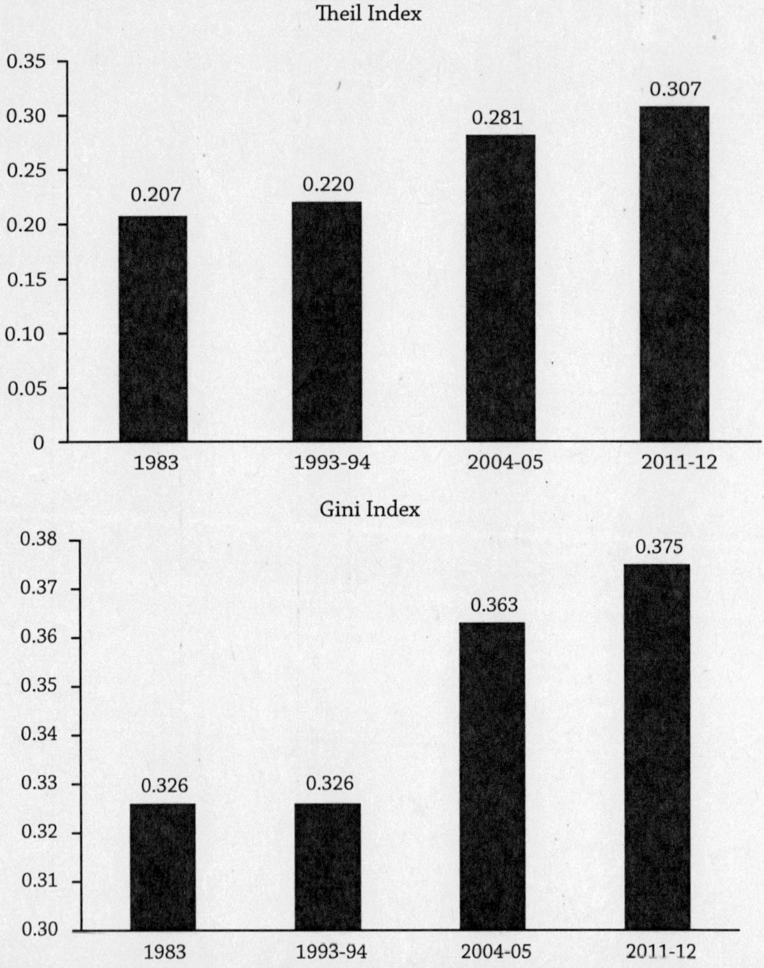

Figure 1.12

Theil Index of Rural and Urban Expenditure Per Capita

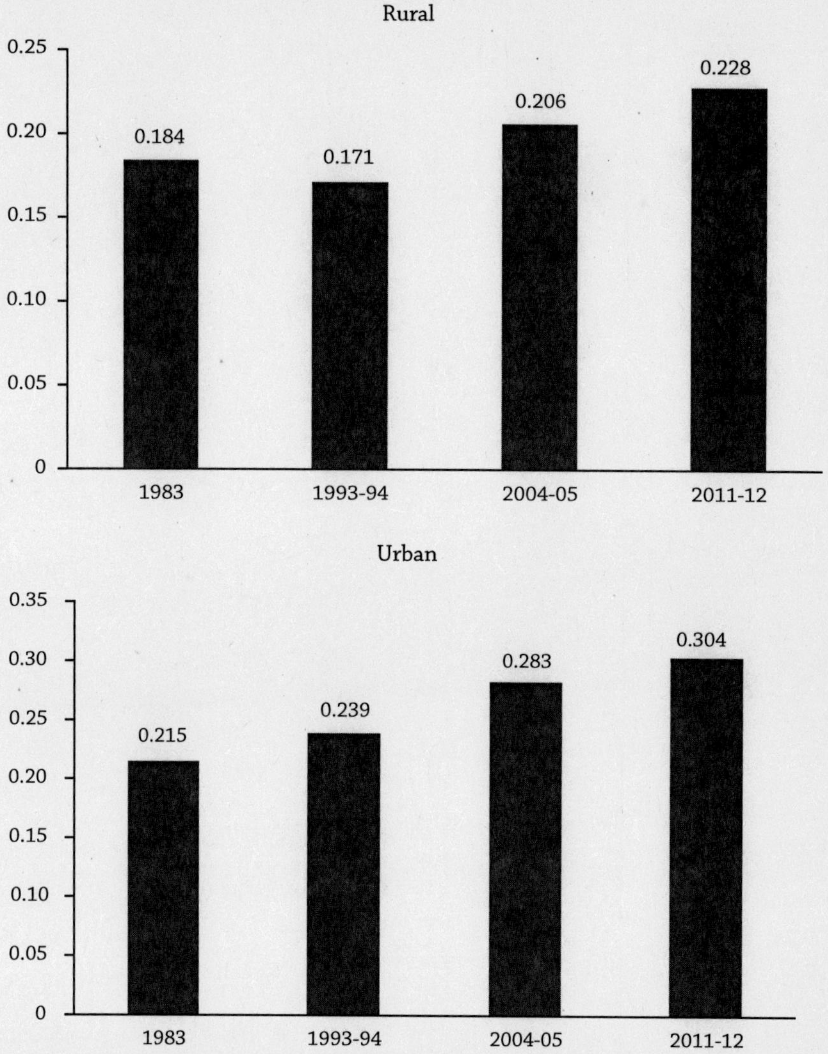

Figure 1.13

Gini Index of Rural and Urban Expenditure Per Capita

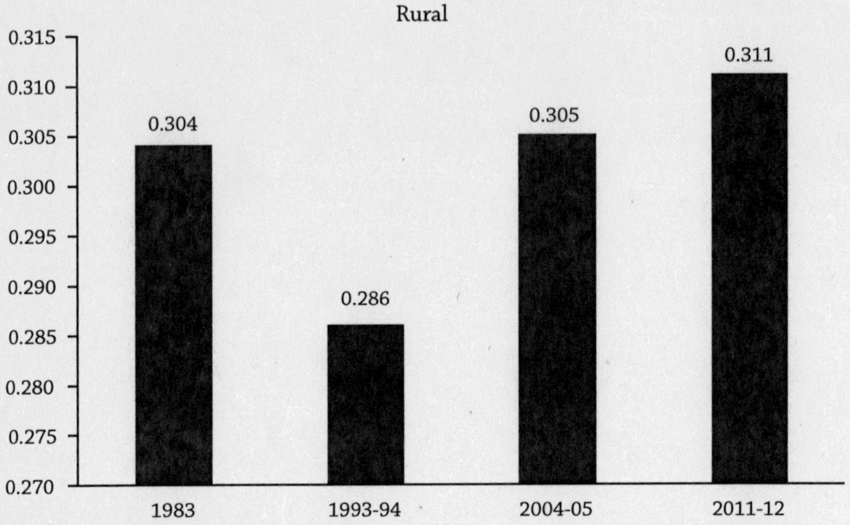

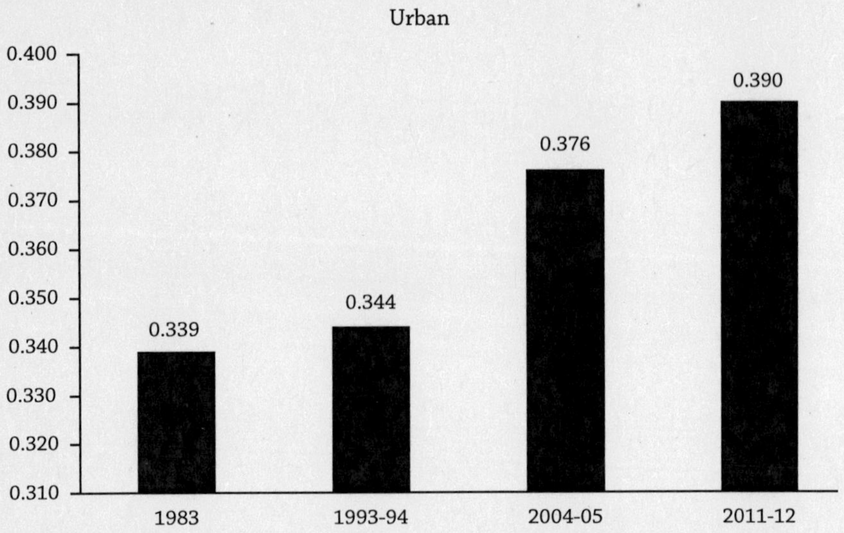

Figure 1.14

10:10 Ratio for Average Monthly Per Capita Expenditure, All India (Ratio of Average Expenditure in Top Decile to Bottom Decile)

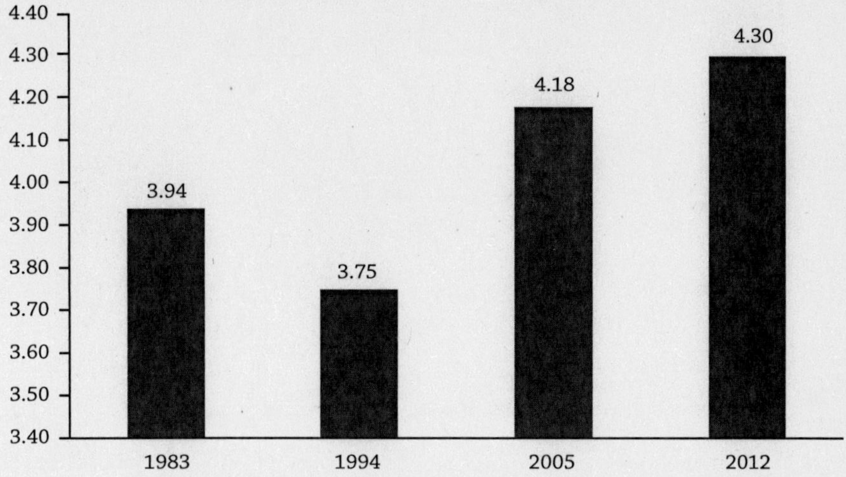

Figure 1.15

10:10 Ratio for Average Monthly Per Capita Expenditure, Rural

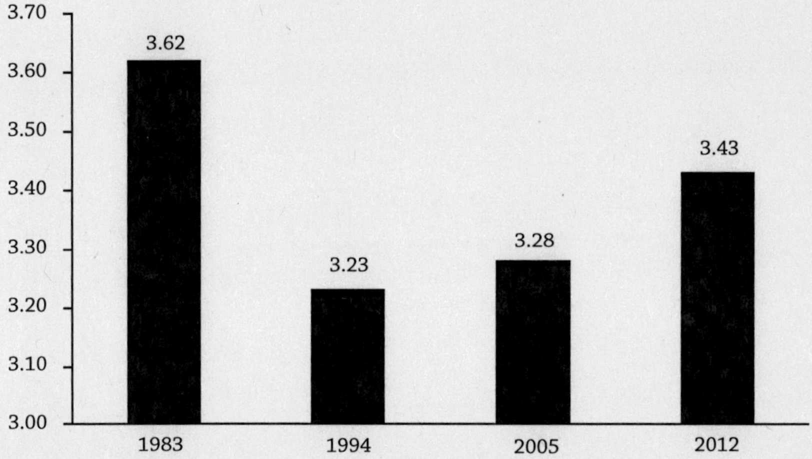

Figure 1.16

10:10 Ratio for Average Monthly Per Capita Expenditure, Urban

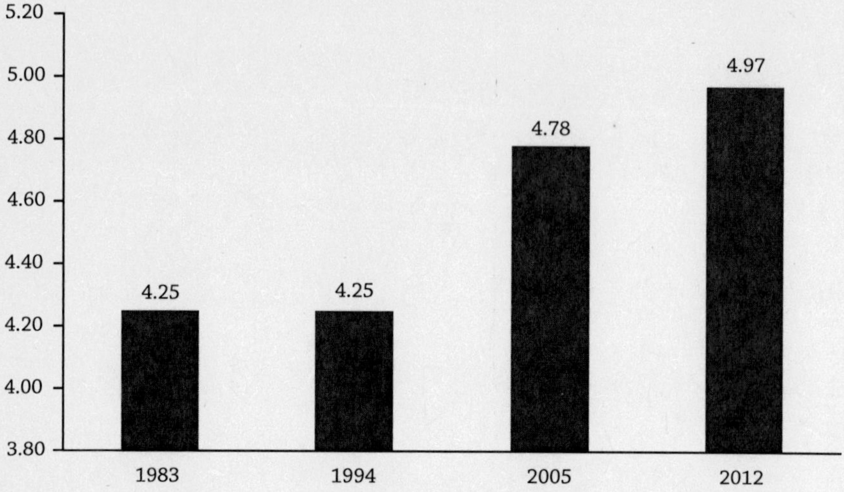

Figure 1.17

Overall Pattern of Distribution of Monthly Per Capita Expenditure (All India)

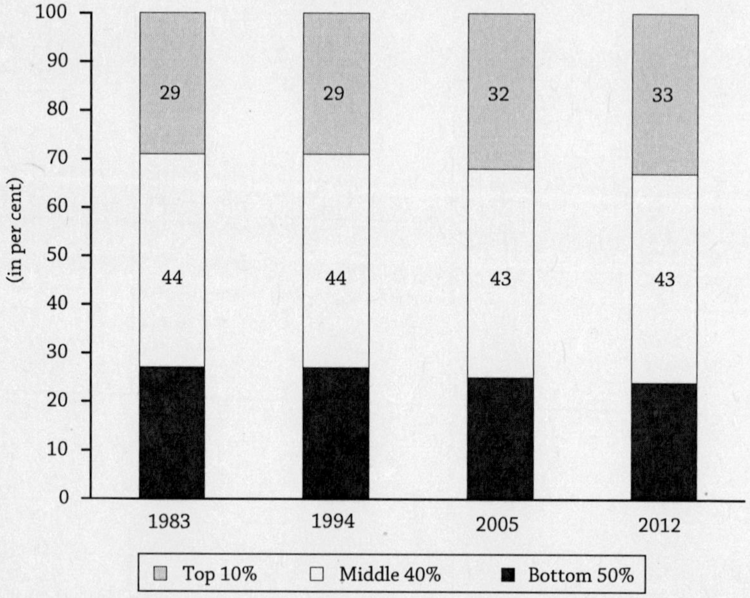

The 10:10 ratios do not show exactly the same pattern (Figures 1.14 to 1.16). The first point to note is that these ratios are much smaller than the corresponding wage ratios—between 3 and 4 in rural areas against 10 to 12 for wages, and between 4 and 5 in urban areas against 16 to 20. That the ratios for consumption are only a quarter of the ratios for wages is partly due to the equalising effect of the consolidation of income within households, though it may also reflect underestimation of expenditure, in particular among higher income groups.

The trend is slightly different from the overall measures. In rural areas, there is a significant drop in the rural ratio in period 1, followed by a rise in periods 2 and 3. This pattern is similar to that for the Gini and Theil indices, but the rise is smaller for the 10:10 ratio. This suggests that the gap between top and bottom in rural areas has not widened as much as might be expected from the overall trend in inequality. In urban areas, on the other hand, the rising trend is very similar to the overall picture shown by the Gini or Theil indices.

Finally the overall pattern of distribution in Figure 1.17 shows a transfer of around 3 percentage points of expenditure from the poorest 50 per cent to the top 10 per cent since 1994, with less change for the middle groups. The change over time is very similar to that for wages, but the share of the top 10 per cent is 7 percentage points less than for wages, and the share of the bottom 40 per cent is 6 percentage points more. As in the case of wages, the stability of the distribution is striking, with only a slow long term trend.

2

Patterns of Wage Inequality

The next step is to explore some of the factors associated with these patterns of and trends in inequality. Of course, the broader forces driving inequality need to be understood in societal and historical context—and that is the subject of a separate publication (Barbosa et al. forthcoming). Here we investigate some of the main characteristics of individuals and jobs that are found in the literature to be strongly associated with wage inequality. Note again that we are obliged, for reasons of data availability, to confine our analysis to waged and salaried workers, excluding the self-employed.

We examine the following factors, which are available from the National Sample Survey (NSS):

1. Work type.
2. Gender.
3. Social group (caste and religion).
4. Education.
5. Region of residence.

We present the pattern of inequality for each of these factors, and investigate their importance in relation to other factors. These factors are not equivalent, even in theory. The first, work type, is a characteristic of labour markets rather than of individuals, and constitutes an endogenous market outcome. Gender and social group are (almost) fixed characteristics of individuals, and so exogenous. Region of residence and education are also characteristic of individuals, but they are not fixed. Region in particular is endogenous through migration, while education is acquired (though essentially fixed once adulthood is reached). Wage differentials across education may be simply a reflection of social hierarchy, in which education plays the role of a mechanism to transmit inequality from one generation to the next. There may, for instance, be a strong interrelation between education and social group, in which social group is in some sense prior to education. These differences need to be borne in mind in interpreting the patterns.

The whole analysis is carried out separately for urban and rural areas. There are considerable differences between rural and urban areas in wages, labour market structures and more generally in social and economic patterns, which imply that the two should not be merged in a single analysis. Of course it is a simplification to treat urban and rural areas as separate. Rural residents have access to urban labour markets through commuting and migration, so the two areas are in reality linked. And there is in reality a graduation from remote rural areas through semi-urban peripheries to large cities, so the distinction between rural and urban areas is just the first step towards understanding a more complex picture.

For analysing inequality under each of these themes, we first consider wage ratios between different categories of worker. Second, we look at the histograms (kernel density functions) of nominal wages and of log wages for different types of work and discuss whether there has been any change over the time on the basis of a visual inspection. It is also interesting to break this down for selected subgroups, notably distinguishing women and men. Third, we decompose wage inequality (the Theil index) by the major categories under each of the themes that we are considering. Subsequently we present some multilevel decompositions, which combine several of these factors. More detailed multivariate analysis is presented in Chapter 4.

Decomposition is a widely used technique to distinguish inequality within particular groups from inequality between them, and the Theil index has the convenient property that it is easily decomposed into additive components. Nevertheless it is easy to over-interpret the results. As Elbers et al. (2008) point out, the "between-group" inequality depends not only on differences in means between the groups, but also on the number of the groups and their relative sizes. If one group is much larger than the others, variation within that group will tend to dominate the results. Moreover, within group inequality using sample survey data reflects not only random variation and a host of unobserved factors, but also measurement error. The fact that the "between" component for a specific variable is small therefore does not mean that it is unimportant. On the other hand, these factors, insofar as they do not change over time, should have less impact on trends. If the "between" component rises or falls over time, it is likely that this reflects in some way a change in the importance of the factor concerned.

It is also important to note that the decomposition of wages misses differential access to different categories of employment, which may lead to labour market exclusion. This is particularly important for women, who may well be excluded from the labour market, or confined to unpaid family labour, which is not captured here, rather than paid lower wages. So wage inequality does not fully capture labour market inequality, for some inequality will be the result of differential access to particular occupations. We will look at wage inequality within occupational groups in Chapter 7 to explore this further.

While an analysis of regional differentials is included here, the patterns can be quite different across Indian states. For certain issues we have therefore looked specifically at three states: Tamil Nadu, Bihar and Punjab. However, for purposes of this monograph we mostly remain at the all-India level. Detailed differences across states merit another paper.

2.1 Work Type

In India, the most basic distinction in the labour market is between casual, daily work (usually daily paid, and usually without written contract or social protection) and regular work (a diverse category which includes both longer term, often monthly paid work without contract or protection, but also regular salaried work in both public and private sector employment. This is now a conventional breakdown, incorporated in NSS and other survey questionnaires. In reality the distinction is not always clear. A lot of 'casual' work is in reality quite regular, in the sense that there is a continuing employment relation, while there are intermediate categories such as contract work where payment may be irregular. Nevertheless this distinction is embedded in the statistics and is the most convenient measure of labour market segmentation.

Figure 2.1 shows the wage ratios between these two types of employment over time.[1] In rural areas, casual wages are of the order of 40 per cent of regular wages. The ratio of mean casual to regular wages fell from 1983 to 2004-05, and then rose again in 2011-12. In urban areas, the difference between casual and regular wages is comparable with that in rural areas, and the overall pattern of change over time—falling and then rising—is also similar, although the amplitude of the change is much less. The main reason for this pattern seems to be a tightening of the market for casual labour after 2004-05, a phenomenon which apparently affects India as a whole, and which is certainly connected with higher GDP (gross domestic product) growth. As for urban-rural differences, there does seem to have been a progressive national integration of the casual wage labour market, which has driven up casual wages in rural areas because these are source areas for urban unskilled migrant labour.

This tightening of the labour market seems to have been a major factor in the reduction of inequality in rural areas after 2004-05, which we noted in the previous chapter.

This ratio concerns the means. But there is a wide variation of wages between individuals. Figure 2.2 gives histograms of log wages for regular and casual workers for our four years.[2] We use log wages because it is easier to see the pattern. These are standardised so that the mean log wage (for all workers) is zero in the figure. In general we can see that:

1. While there is substantial variation for both regular and casual work, it is larger for regular wages, which reflects a wider variety of work situations. Casual wages are more concentrated, as can be seen from the higher bars.

1. A number of assumptions are made in the collection and reporting of the data to convert salaries of regular workers to an equivalent daily payment. Some of these assumptions can be questioned (see for instance Ghose 2014) but for purposes of this analysis we use the NSS figures.
2. These histograms exclude the top 1 per cent of the distribution and wages recorded as zero, some of which may be errors or might concern special situations.

2. While there is a large difference in the means between the two groups, they overlap considerably. Casual wages tend to be concentrated in the range -2 standard deviations (of log wages) to +1; regular wages in the range -1 to +2. But for both a high proportion of observations are in the range -1 to +1 standard deviation.

Figure 2.1

Ratio of Casual to Regular Wages

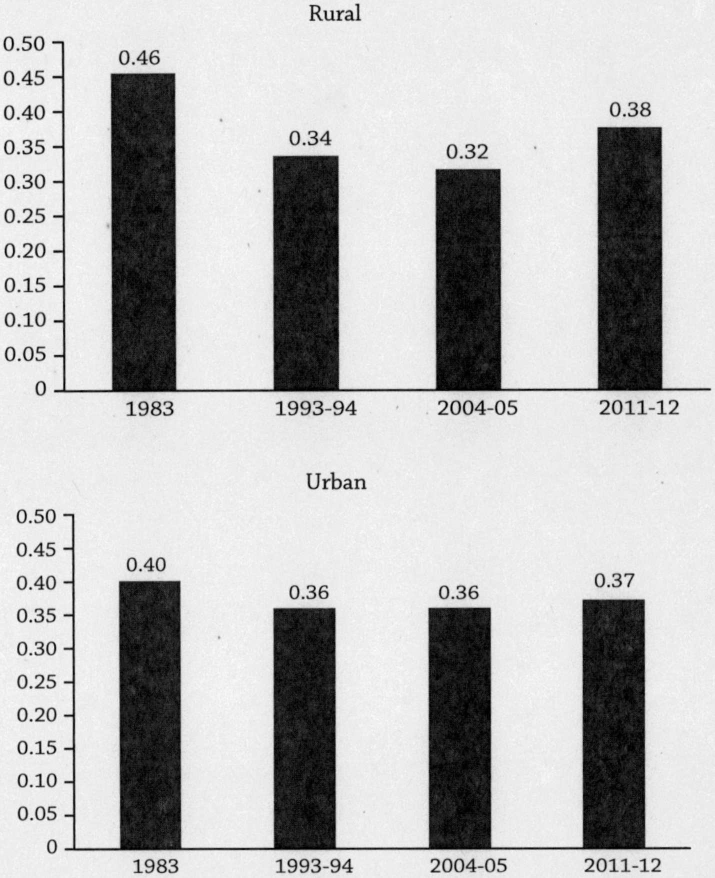

Figure 2.2

Histograms of Log Nominal Wages (Standardised, and Excluding Top 1 Per Cent of the Distribution and Zeros), 1983 to 2011-12

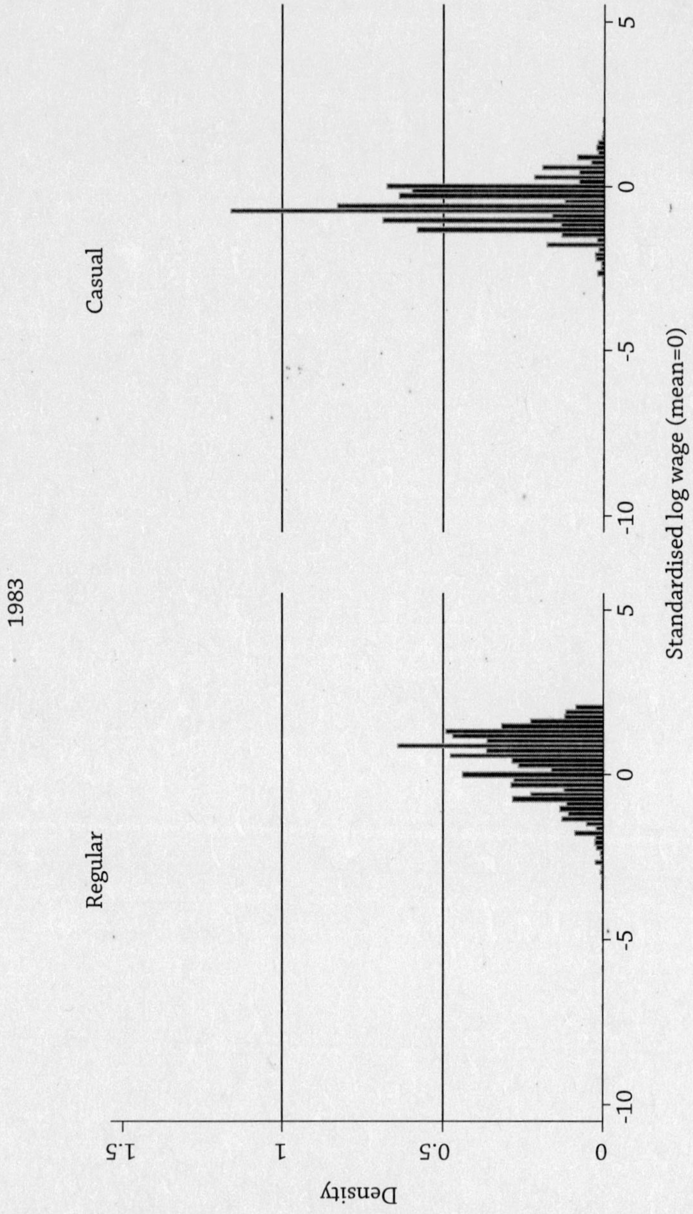

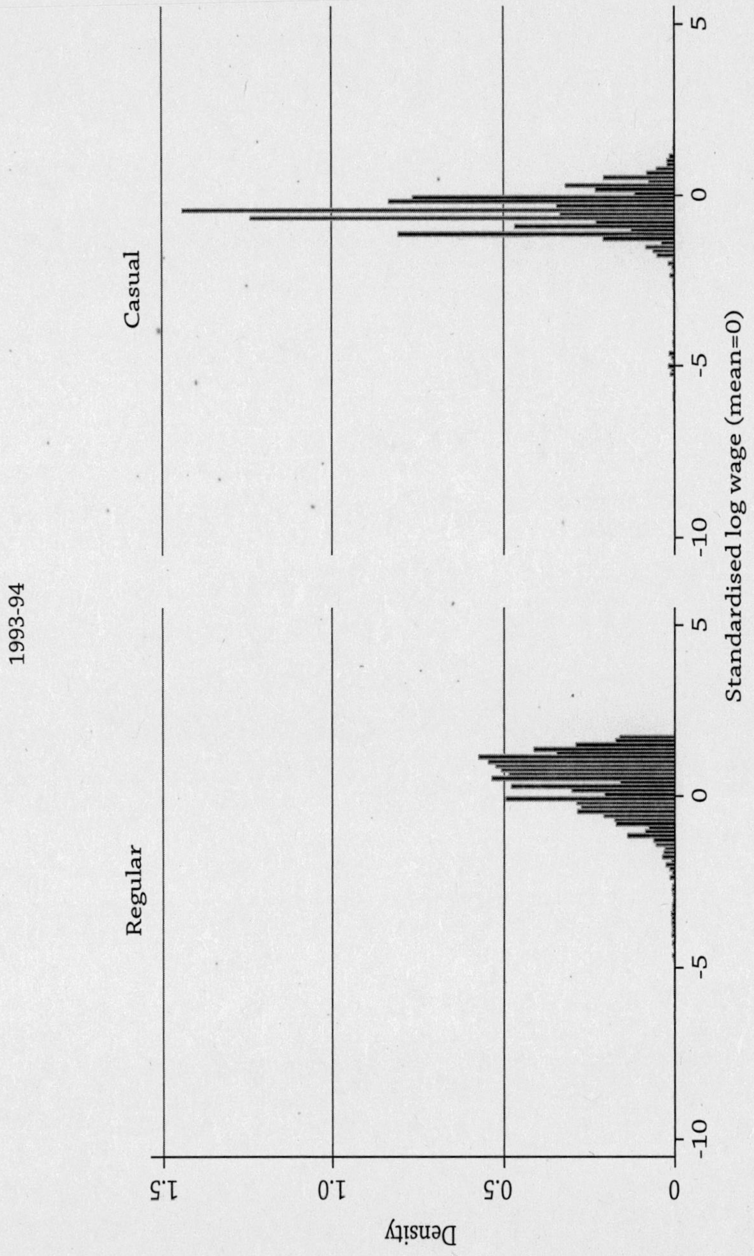
1993-94
Regular
Casual
Density
0
0.5
1.0
1.5
-10
-5
0
5
-10
-5
0
5
Standardised log wage (mean=0)

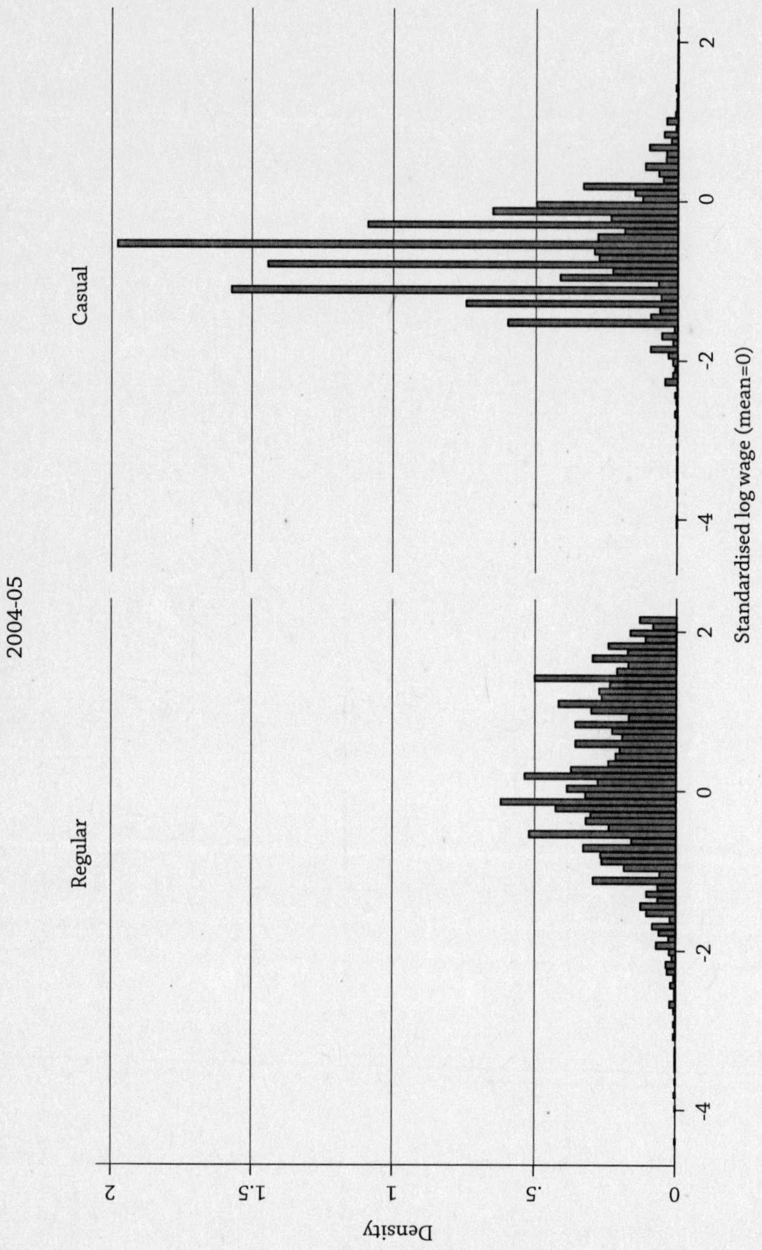
2004-05
Regular
Casual
Density
0
.5
1
1.5
2
-4
-2
0
2
Standardised log wage (mean=0)

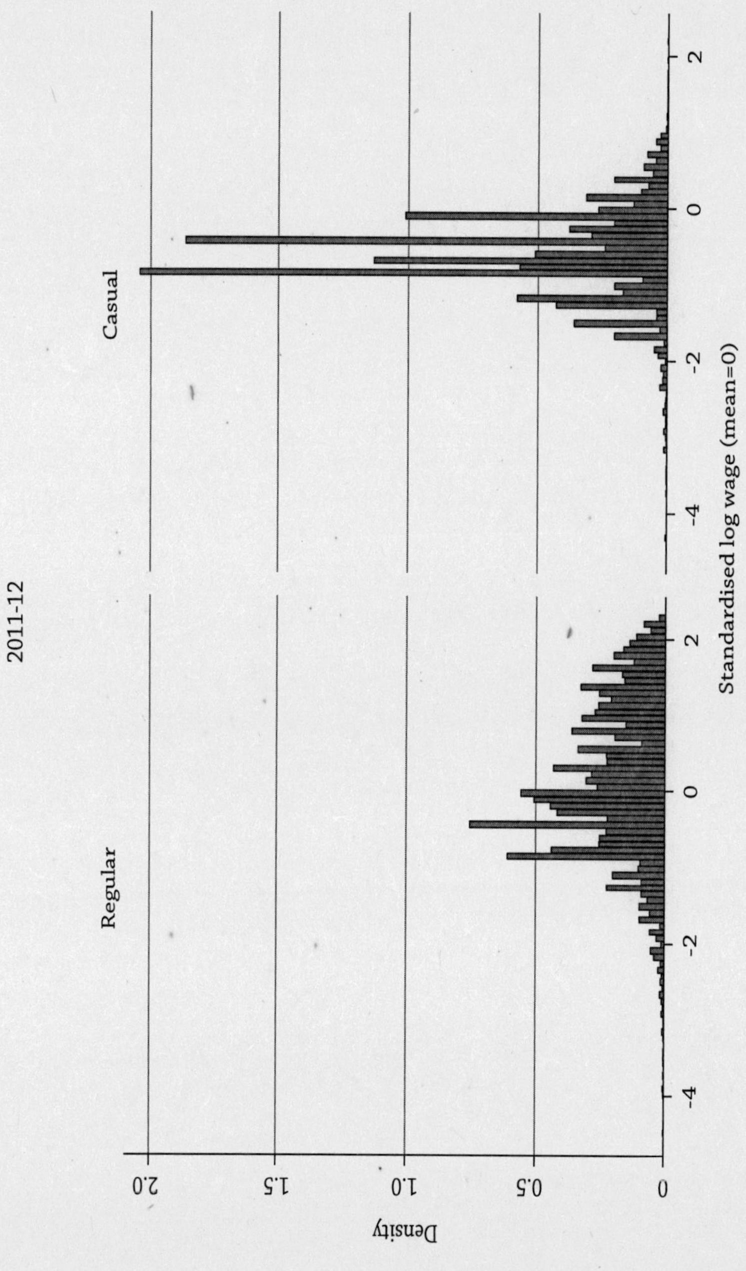
2011-12
Regular
Casual
Density
0
0.5
1.0
1.5
2.0
-4
-2
0
2
Standardised log wage (mean=0)

3. While changes in the pattern over time are hard to isolate visually (note that the scale for the first two years is different from the last two years), casual wages can be seen to have become more concentrated, while regular wages have become more dispersed. This is in fact borne out by the Gini coefficients of wage inequality, which fell fairly sharply for casual work in both urban and rural areas (from 0.33 to 0.27 in rural and from 0.35 to 0.29 in urban areas), but which rose for regular work from 0.36 to 0.47 in urban areas, and from 0.43 to 0.44 in rural areas.

We might infer that the observed growth in inequality in urban areas at least comes in part from an increasing dispersion of regular wages. This would be particularly true of the period from 1993-94 to 2004-05, when the ratio of casual to regular wages did not change much. In the period since 2004-05 rising dispersion of regular wages was compensated by the increase in casual wages relative to regular.

We then decompose the Theil measure of inequality (see the discussion above) by work type (Figure 2.3). It can be seen that the "between" component, that is to say the difference between regular and casual wages, accounts for a substantial proportion of all wage inequality. In rural areas, it rises from 19 per cent in 1983 to 34 per cent in 1993-94. This was a period when the ratio of mean casual to regular wages declined from 0.43 to 0.38, which is no doubt an important explanation. Thereafter the contribution of the between component declined, especially after 2004-05, reflecting the opposite factor of a rise in mean casual wages in relation to regular. But the difference between the two types of work still accounts for almost a quarter of inequality in 2011-12.

In urban areas the pattern of change over time is somewhat similar, but less marked, and by 2011-12 the casual:regular difference accounts for only 12 per cent of wage inequality. However, this can largely be explained by the smaller fluctuations in the casual:regular wage ratio in urban than in rural areas. Increased dispersion of regular wages, as noted above, probably also played a role—since as this becomes more important in inequality the contribution of the casual: regular differential declines.

Figure 2.3

Decomposition of Wage Inequality Across Regular and Casual Workers

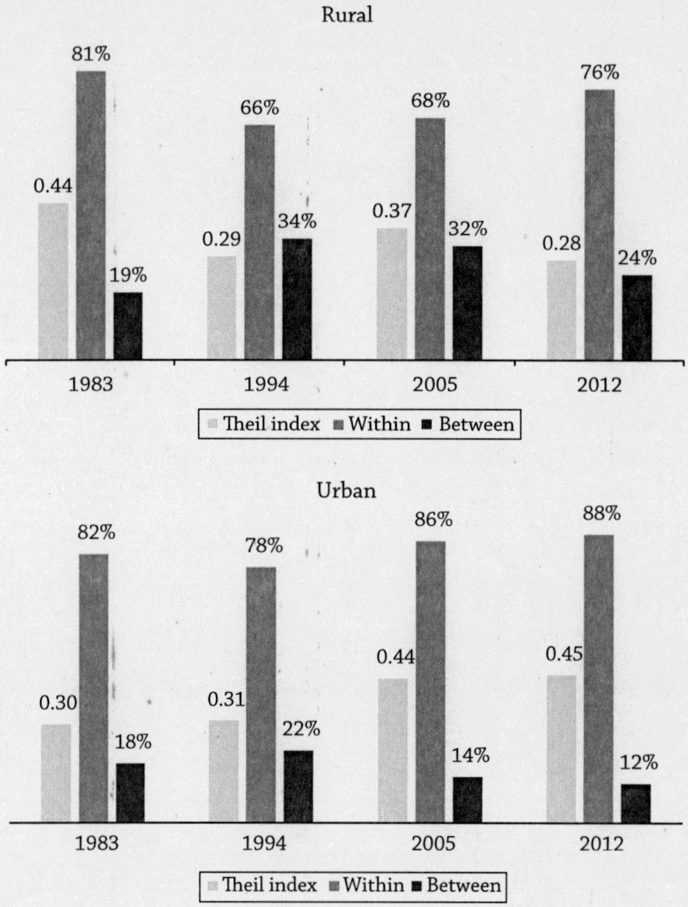

To sum up, the segmentation of the labour market into casual and regular work makes a substantial contribution to wage inequality overall, but one which is more important in rural than in urban areas, and which has been declining since 1994. The decline in the importance of this segmentation reflects both the increasing dispersion within regular work (reducing the relative importance of the casual-regular differential), and more recently both an increase in the share of regular work and a tightening of the market for casual labour which has reduced wage differentials.

2.2 Gender

Women's wages are much lower than men's, on average, but the overall ratio has been rising, from 0.5 in 1983 to 0.7 in 2011-12 (Figure 2.4). However, this has not been a uniform improvement, since it results from the combination of a number of different factors.

As can be seen from Figure 2.4, the female:male wage ratios for each type of work—regular and casual, urban and rural—show a much less consistent trend than for the labour market as a whole. While the ratio has risen in three of the four categories, the rise is less and less regular than the overall figure. The change in the overall ratio therefore has to reflect a shift in the pattern of women's employment towards types of work where the wage differential with men is lower.

Figure 2.4

Ratio of Female to Male Wages for Different Work Categories, Urban and Rural, 1983 to 2011-12

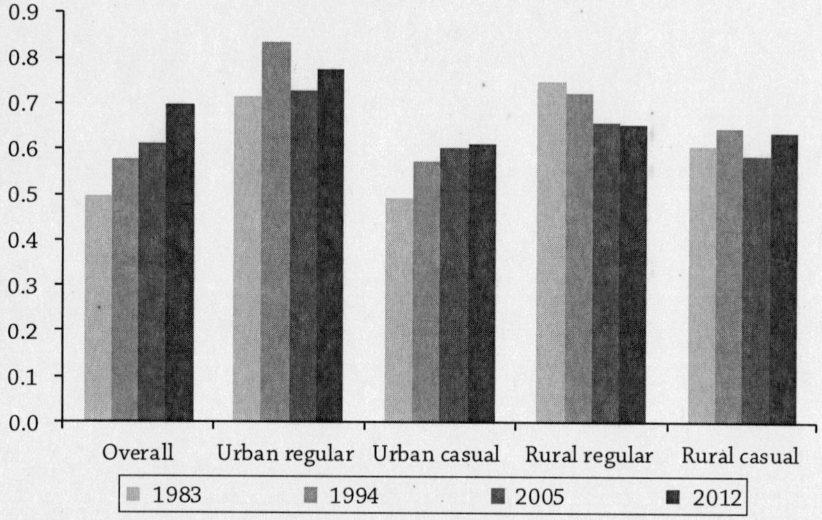

This shift can be clearly seen in Table 2.1. In 1983 women were heavily concentrated in casual rural work, to a much greater extent than men, 44 per cent of whom were in regular work in either urban or rural areas, as against 17 per cent of women. Over time, these disparities decreased. By 2011-12, 22 per cent of women were in regular urban work, still less than men at 27 per cent but the gap had closed. The same was true in rural areas. There was a corresponding sharper decline in the dependence of women on casual wage employment. So although gender inequality in the type of job remained, it had been reduced—and this was clearly reflected in the reduction in the overall wage disparity, a reduction that was greater overall than for individual categories of wage employment. Nevertheless, it should also be noted that women's share of wage workers declined from 28 per cent in 1983 to 23 in 2011-12. So while some of the decline in casual rural work was replaced by regular work at a higher wage, a significant proportion was replaced by withdrawal from the labour force, which of course does not appear in the wage data. So the improvement in the labour market situation of women is exaggerated by these data.

Table 2.1

Distribution of Male and Female Wage Workers Across Regular-Casual and Urban-Rural Categories, 1983 to 2011-12 (%)

	1983		*1993-94*		*2004-05*		*2011-12*	
	Male	*Female*	*Male*	*Female*	*Male*	*Female*	*Male*	*Female*
Regular urban	25	9	24	11	25	16	27	22
Casual urban	8	9	8	8	8	6	9	7
Regular rural	19	8	15	7	16	10	15	13
Casual rural	49	74	52	73	51	68	49	58
Total	100	100	100	100	100	100	100	100
Distribution of all workers by sex (%)	72	28	72	28	73	27	77	23

Note: This table uses CWS (current weekly status) to measure work, i.e. based on whether an economic activity was done in the seven days prior to the survey. NSS has four different measures of employment, of which the most commonly used is UPSS (usual principal and subsidiary status). We use CWS because the wage data refer to the same seven day reference period. CWS tends to give lower levels of employment than UPSS, especially for women.

To fully understand the pattern we also need to understand the nature of women's regular work. In rural areas, for instance, it tends to be dominated by teaching and health work. Men have a wider range of options. In that case the trends in the wage ratio between men and women depend mainly on which types of jobs are expanding. We need to break this down by occupation to understand it properly.

In urban casual work there is a clear, systematic upward trend in the wage ratio, from 0.48 to over 0.6. This can probably be understood in terms of the gradual exhaustion of the unskilled labour surplus. In rural areas the pattern is not so strong, though the trend is still upwards in the recent period. Women in rural labour markets are less well integrated into the national labour market because they are less able to migrate than men, on the whole.

Histograms of the wage distribution also suggest something that cannot be observed in the averages. As Figure 2.5 shows, in 1983, while the distribution of male and female wages overlap, men visibly predominate at the upper end of the scale for all categories of work, casual and regular and urban and rural. In 2012 this is no longer the case in regular work. As many women as men are found at the upper end of the scale. But men predominate in the mid levels and women at the bottom. The distribution for women is almost bimodal. This is less true for casual work, which has changed much less.

The decomposition of inequality by gender is interesting and in some respects puzzling too. In rural areas, the contribution to inequality of sex differences in wages has fluctuated, with a peak at 11 per cent in 1993-94 and a minimum of 5 per cent in 2011-12 (Figure 2.6). In urban areas, however, the contribution of gender differences declines steadily, to no more than 1 per cent in 2011-12. It is plausible that the contribution of sex differences in wages to inequality has declined, but not so much, since a considerable gap in mean wages persists.

This turns out to be at least in part a compositional effect, because when we separate casual and regular work the effects are quite different. Figure 2.7 shows that for casual workers alone, sex differences continue to account for a significant proportion of overall inequality in both urban and rural areas, although declining in both since 2004-05. For regular workers, on the other hand, the contribution of gender is small, with no clear overall trend. It should be noted that the bimodal pattern of the wage distribution for women will not be picked up in this type of decomposition, so differences in gender patterns can still be important. And of course, we are only discussing wages here. There are well known differences in labour market access for men and women, to the disadvantage of the women.

2.3 Inequality Between Social Groups

In India there are strong reasons to expect wage inequalities across a variety of social groups, for labour markets are segmented and caste and religion are important factors in this segmentation, facilitating and legitimising it where they do not cause it.

However, the notion of a social group is a flexible one, and the role played by different caste groups has changed over time. In the NSS the only consistent distinction has been that between SCs (scheduled castes) and STs (scheduled tribes) on the one hand, and all others, reflecting the recognition in India's Constitution of the disadvantage suffered by the former groups. This breakdown is available since 1983. Starting in the 1980s, there was a wider recognition of the notion of OBCs (other backward classes), leading eventually to reservations for this group in public sector employment and educational institutions.[3] Subsequently OBCs were also identified in the NSS questionnaire, but only as from the 2004-05 survey.

The caste breakdown intersects with the breakdown by religion. The largest group other than Hindus, Muslims, also needs to be separated out because labour markets are to some degree segmented by religion. In addition, there is now an admitted distinction among Muslims between OBCs and others—the latter, like the 'other' Hindus, tend to be better off groups. In addition there are a number of other religious minorities in India, including Christians, Buddhists, Sikhs, and other smaller groups, some of them quite regionally concentrated.

All of these different identities are associated with differences in access to employment; indeed the original foundation of caste is occupational segmentation, even if it is much diluted today. Some identities are also a source of direct discrimination. In order to explore how far these factors influence wage inequality, we have looked at two breakdowns, both a simplification of a complex reality.

---

3. See Barbosa et al (forthcoming) for more discussion of this issue.

Figure 2.5

Histogram of Standardised Nominal Log Wages Across Gender and Work Type, 'Rural and Urban'

1983

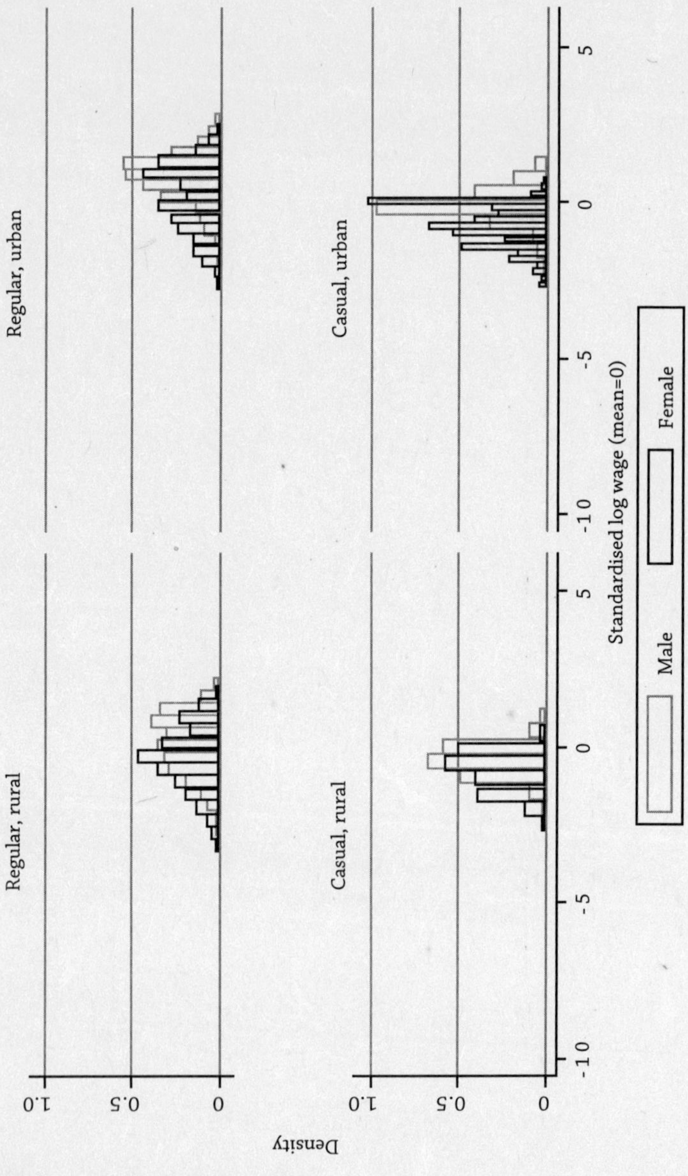

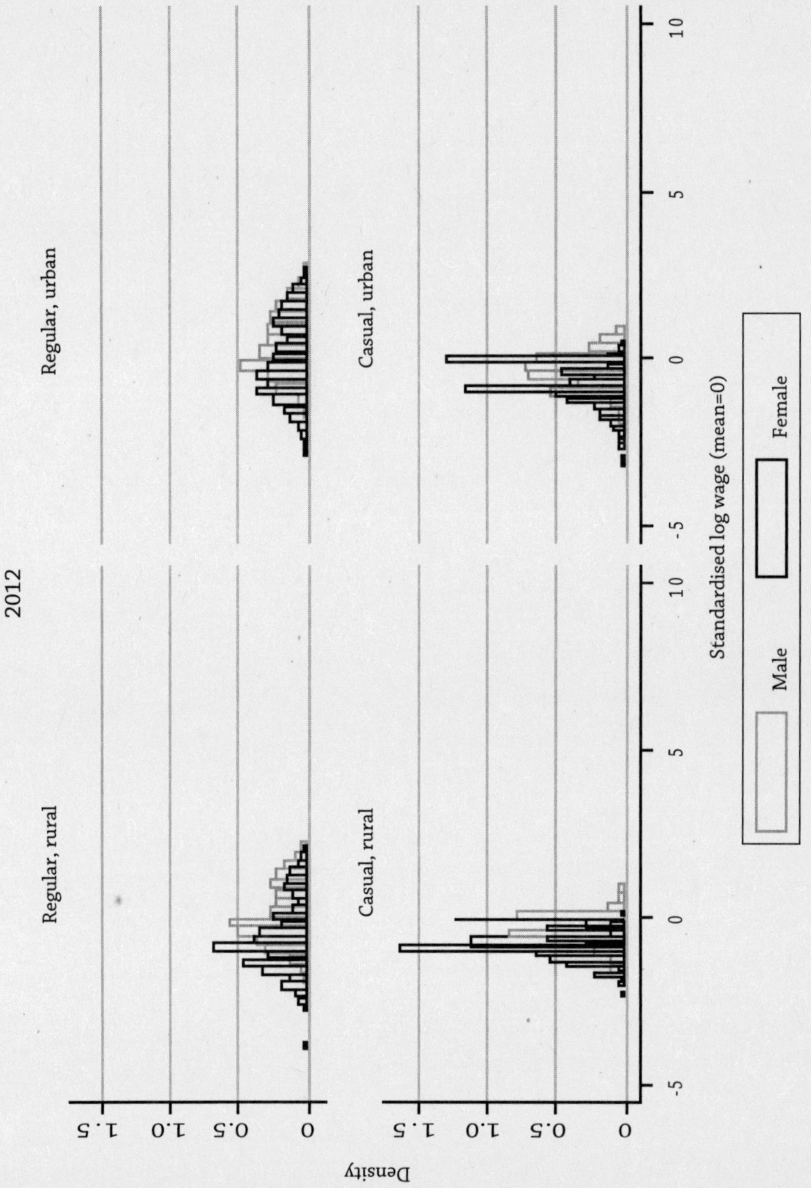
2012
Regular, rural
Regular, urban
Casual, rural
Casual, urban
Density
Standardised log wage (mean=0)
Male
Female

Figure 2.6

Decompositions of Wage Inequality by Sex

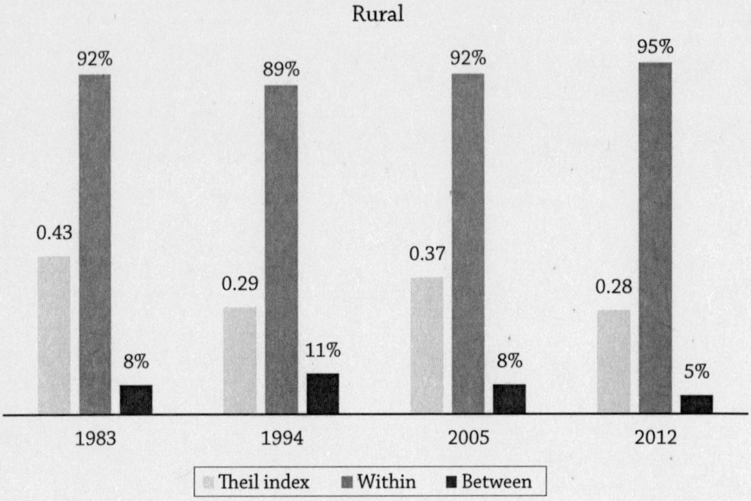

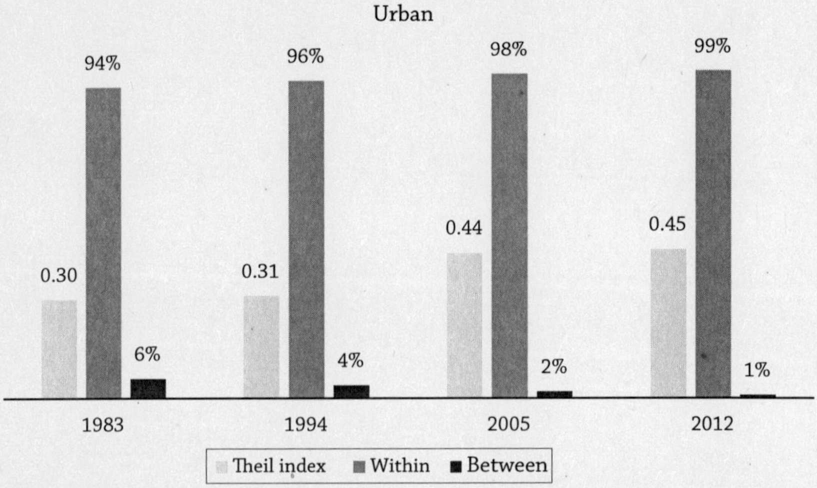

The first merely distinguishes SCs and STs from the rest. There are of course important differences between SCs and STs in way of life and labour market integration, but we neglect those for the moment. This distinction can be maintained in the four rounds of the NSS that we are using.

Figure 2.7

Decomposition of Wage Inequality by Sex

Casual Workers

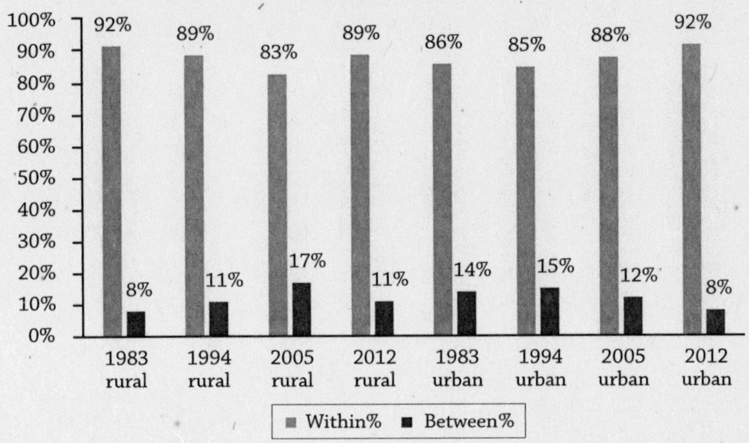

Regular Workers

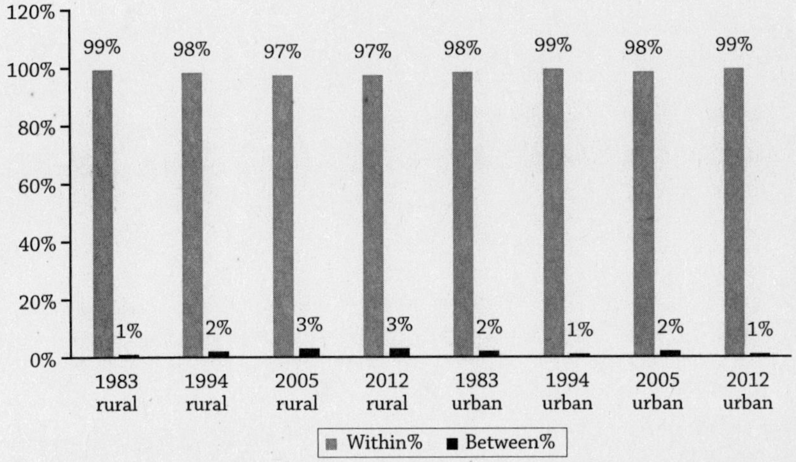

The second tries to capture some more complex patterns. We can identify the following groups for the 2004-05 and 2011-12 surveys:

- Scheduled Tribe.
- Scheduled Caste.
- Hindu OBC (which despite the name includes both lower and middle castes).

- Hindu: other caste (mainly upper castes).
- Muslim OBC.
- Muslim: other (mainly upper groups).
- Other religion.

Figure 2.8 shows the wage ratios for all other groups in relation to SC/ST, for rural and urban areas, since 1983. It can be seen that the overall differential remains high in 2011-12, 27 per cent in rural areas and 43 per cent in urban, and slightly higher overall (55%) because SC and ST tend to be concentrated in lower wage rural areas. But there is some sign that the ratio, after fluctuating between 1983 and 2005 with little clear trend, has started to come down. It fell by about 8 per cent in rural areas, 4 per cent in urban areas and 9 per cent overall between 2005 and 2012. This pattern can largely be traced to the improvement in the relative position of casual workers, where STs and SCs are overrepresented (as discussed below).

Figure 2.8

Wage Ratios for Social Groups (Others: SC/ST)

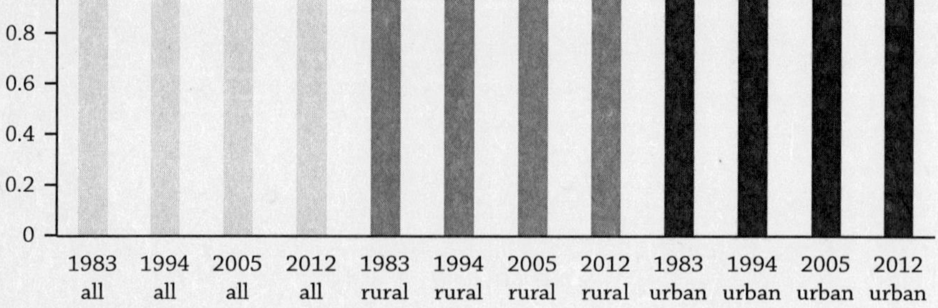

Despite the relatively high wage ratios, the decomposition (Figure 2.9) indicates that the contribution to overall inequality of this

division between SC/ST and the rest is quite small—of the order of 2 to 3 per cent, with a decline visible in the last year.

Figure 2.9

Decomposition of Inequality for Social Groups (SC/ST and Others)

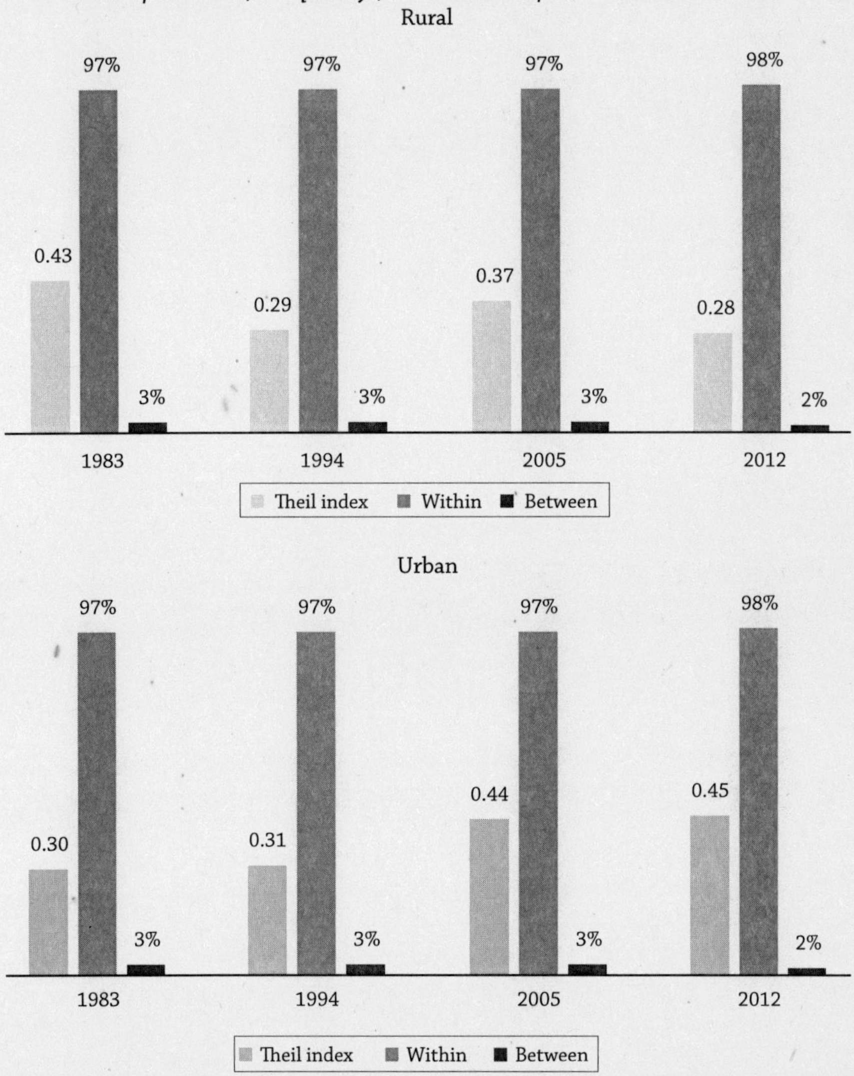

The more detailed classification of social groups shows that there are important differences between other groups as well as those between SC/ST and others. It can be seen in Figure 2.10 that Hindu OBCs have higher wages than SCs, but the difference is not large and there is no clear trend, nor is there much difference between rural and urban areas. There is not much difference between Hindu OBCs and Muslim OBCs either, although there is some sign of the gap increasing between 2004-05 and 2011-12, especially in urban areas. The gap between "other" (upper) Hindus and Hindu OBCs is quite considerable, a wage ratio of 2 overall. It is lower in rural areas and showing some tendency to decline, but in urban areas it is stable. The ratio between "other" Hindus and "other" Muslims (i.e. the upper groups in the social stratification for both religions) is also high, stable overall, declining in rural areas but increasing in urban areas. In reality upper Muslim groups do not seem to be advantaged compared with Muslim OBCs in wage employment.

Figure 2.10

Wage Ratios for Socio-Religious Groups (More Detailed Definition)

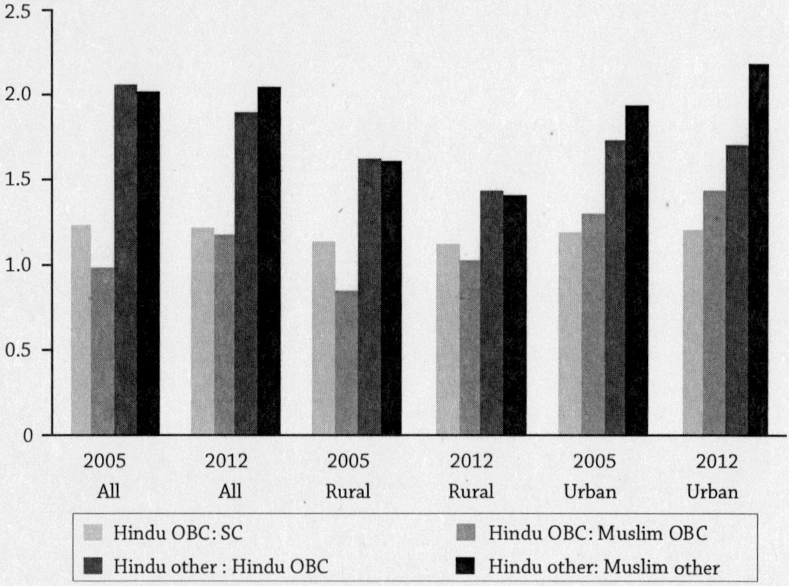

Table 2.2 shows the pattern of wage employment for these social groups in 2011-12. It is apparent that wage differentials may be

less important than inequality in access to good jobs. STs and SCs are concentrated in casual rural employment, where wages are low, while over half of upper caste Hindus are found in urban regular work. Muslims and OBCs are in an intermediate position. These differentials seem to be quite stable over time. In 1983 some 22 per cent of wage work among Scheduled Castes and Tribes was regular; by 2011-12 this had risen only to 26 per cent. Meanwhile, for all others the percent of regular work had risen from 46 to 58 per cent.

Table 2.2

Pattern of Employment for Each Socio-Religious Group, 2011-12

(% distribution)

Work Type	*ST*	*SC*	*Hindu OBC*	*Hindu-Upper*	*Muslim-OBC*	*Muslim-Upper*	*Other Religion*
Urban regular	9	16	23	51	22	27	34
Urban casual	5	8	9	5	16	13	7
Rural regular	10	11	15	20	14	14	20
Rural casual	76	65	53	24	48	46	39
Total	100	100	100	100	100	100	100

The decomposition results (Figure 2.11), using this broader social breakdown, gives much more influence to social group than we found when we only distinguished between SC/ST and others. In 2011 this accounted for 13 per cent of wage inequality overall, and 6 per cent in rural and 11 per cent in urban. There was some decline in the importance of social group in rural areas and overall between 2005 and 2012. It is interesting to note that social group is a more important factor in urban than in rural areas, since this is contrary to the common assumption that caste and religion play a larger role in rural society.

Because the influence of social group interacts with other factors, it is useful to break it down further. Table 2.3 gives the contribution of social group to wage inequality within regular and casual work, and for women and men. The results show that social group is a more important influence on wages in regular than in casual work in urban areas, while the reverse is true in rural areas. Since it is urban regular work that generates the highest incomes, this is a significant difference. Moreover, the effect is particularly strong for women, in both urban and rural areas. This no doubt is because of the type of regular work to which women have access. High caste women may well have access to professional jobs, while low caste women are more likely to be found in domestic service. In contrast, very few high caste women will be found in casual work. So the pattern of inequality results from the interaction between these three factors—sex, social group and type of work.

Figure 2.11

Decomposition of Wage Inequality Across Social Groups (More Detailed)

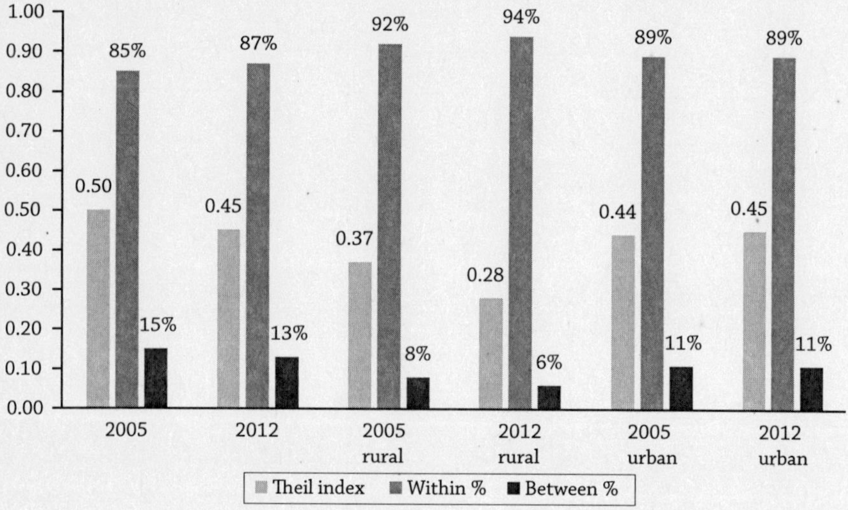

One of the difficulties of analysing the impact of social identity on inequality in India is that the pattern of castes and their hierarchy varies a great deal from state to state. In some states upper castes dominate the economic system, in others they are marginal. Backward classes are very important in some states. The proportion of Muslims varies greatly, while other religions are important in some states, such as Sikhs in Punjab and Christians in the Northeast. By aggregating these different situations into a national picture, we are often mixing apples and oranges. In reality we need to look at the decompositions or ratios at the state level, where we can expect the effect to be stronger as a result of local factors. Data for three states, Bihar, Tamil Nadu and Punjab illustrate this point.

Table 2.3

Contribution of Social Group to Theil Index by Work Type and Sex (%)

Work Type	*Sex*	*2004-05*	*2011-12*
Rural regular	All	4	3
	Female	8	6
	Male	4	3
Rural casual	All	6	4
	Female	2	2
	Male	6	4
Urban regular	All	8	7
	Female	12	10
	Male	8	6
Urban casual	All	4	3
	Female	3	3
	Male	4	3

The wage decomposition for Bihar (Table 2.4), supports this argument about local factors. The contribution of social group to the Theil index rises quite sharply in both rural and urban areas after 1993-94. This coincides with the political and economic rise of the middle castes in that state, though other factors may also be involved.[4]

In Tamil Nadu, the contribution of social group to inequality in rural areas is close to 20 per cent, and quite constant over time. In urban areas it is much lower, and declining, from 5 to 3 per cent. This is the classic pattern one would expect in a modernising society, and very different from what is observed in Bihar.

4. Table 2.4, which is just an illustration, uses a different definition of social group. More regional level analysis would be needed to analyse these issues further.

Table 2.4

Wage Decompositions by Social Group for Selected States

	Year	*Theil Index*	*Within*	*Between*
		Bihar		
Rural	1994	0.32	98%	2%
	2005	0.27	94%	8%
	2012	0.25	91%	9%
Urban	1994	0.34	96%	4%
	2005	0.52	95%	5%
	2012	0.45	82%	18%
		Tamil Nadu		
Rural	1994	0.26	81%	19%
	2005	0.27	83%	17%
	2012	0.19	82%	18%
Urban	1994	0.35	95%	5%
	2005	0.45	95%	5%
	2012	0.33	97%	3%
		Punjab		
Rural	1994	0.13	99%	1%
	2005	0.36	99%	1%
	2012	0.24	97%	3%
Urban	1994	0.22	99%	1%
	2005	0.39	99%	1%
	2012	0.44	>99%	<1%
		Haryana		
Rural	1994	1994	91%	9%
	2005	0.59	96%	4%
	2012	0.22	98%	2%
Urban	1994	0.31	97%	3%
	2005	0.28	>99%	<1%
	2012	0.52	>99%	<1%

In Punjab, on the other hand, the contribution of social group is small in both urban and rural areas, with no obvious trend. This reflects the very different social make up of Punjab. Meanwhile, in

Haryana, the contribution is larger than in Punjab (though still less than in Tamil Nadu and Bihar) and shows a distinct trend, higher in rural than in urban areas, and declining in both, to very low levels in urban areas.

These state-wise results show how risky it is to read too much into the national figures. The trends and patterns in different parts of the country are entirely different.

2.4 Education

To examine the contribution of education to wage differentials we used the following classification:

1. Illiterate (no schooling) (32%).
2. Below primary or literate without schooling (18%).
3. Primary completed (14%).
4. Middle school completed (14%).
5. Secondary or higher secondary completed (16%).
6. Graduates and other tertiary education (7%).

Figures in brackets are the percentages of the population in each category in 2011-12, according to NSS data. Figure 2.12 shows the wage ratios between different educational categories for our four survey years. There is an interesting and very clear pattern. The premium to education is everywhere above one, indicating that more education is reflected in higher wages. But the premium for all schooling levels below middle school is falling over time. Thus, the wage premium for minimal schooling or literacy, as compared with illiteracy, has fallen from 45 to 13 per cent, and there is now little additional gain from completing primary or middle school (only 6%). In contrast, the premium to secondary and college education (and above) is higher. The premium to secondary and higher secondary increased up to 2004-05, falling in 2011-12 but still 47 per cent compared with middle school. Meanwhile, the returns to tertiary education are increasing rapidly. The premium to college education over secondary/higher secondary has risen from 50 to 137 per cent over the 30 year period. This shows the upward shift in the educational credentials demanded by the labour market. Secondary schooling is no longer sufficient to deliver a substantial wage premium; it is necessary to move up the scale. Even at the bottom of the scale, primary education conveys very little labour market advantage any more.

Figure 2.12

Wage Ratios Across Different Education Categories

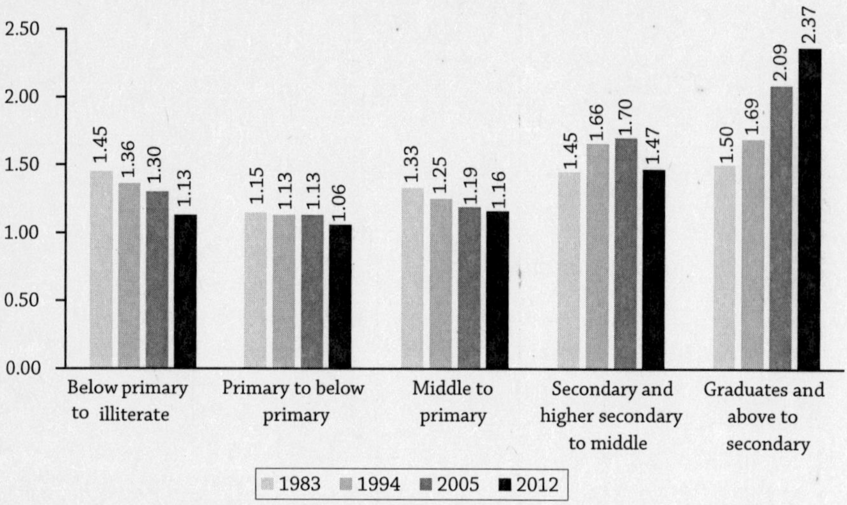

Decompositions of wages across education groups (Figure 2.13) show that the between component is large (generally over 30%), and increasing up to 2004-05 in both urban and rural areas, with a decline thereafter. As expected, the contribution is larger in urban than in rural areas, although the difference is less than might be expected. This is in line with the usual results from decomposition of wages by education. This is sometimes interpreted as a direct effect of education, but the reality is not straightforward since access to education is differentiated by social group, sex and other factors, so that a difference in wages which is associated with differences in education may in fact reflect deeper social forces. We discuss this further when analysing multivariate relationships in Chapter 4.

Figure 2.13

Decomposition of Wages Across Education Categories, Rural and Urban

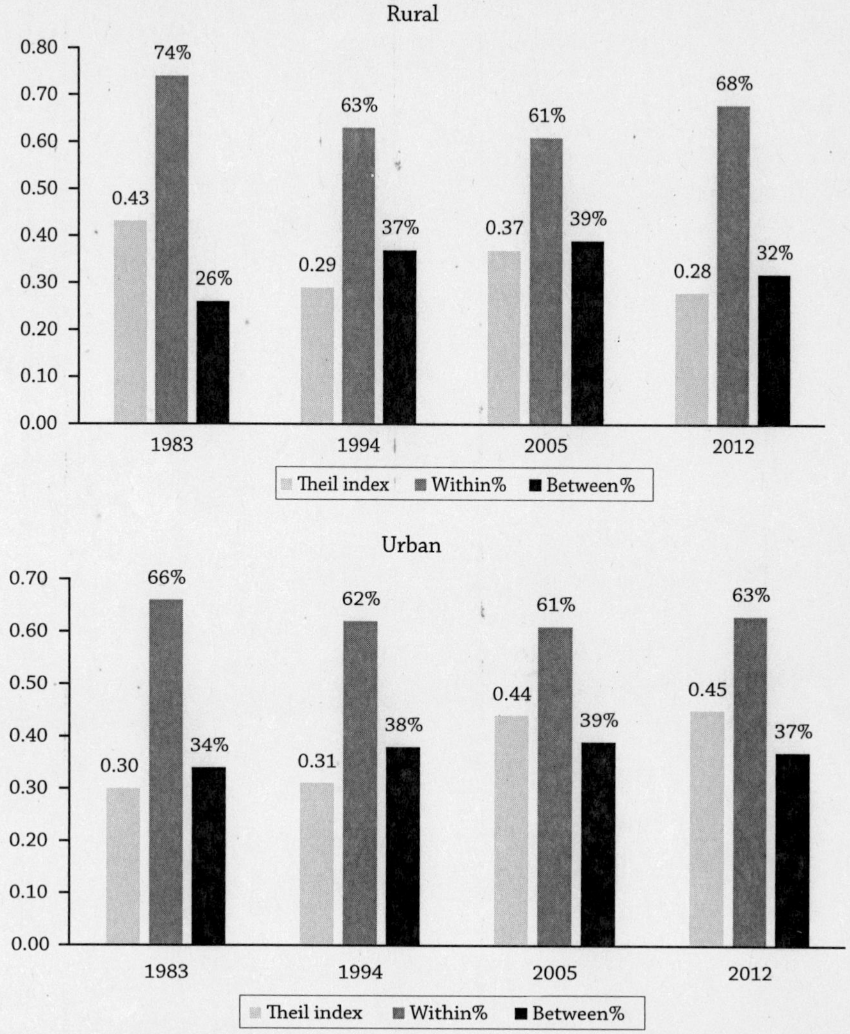

But the influence of education is very uneven across different segments of the labour market, as can be seen in Table 2.5, which shows the contribution of the "between education groups" component for the Theil index, broken down by rural-urban, regular-casual work and sex. First of all, there is a huge difference in the contribution of education to wage differentials between regular and casual work. In regular work the contribution is in the range 20 to 45 per cent, whereas for most casual categories it is less than 5 per cent. For women in casual work in rural areas, education makes virtually no contribution at all. Second, the contribution of education in regular work is as important for women as for men, on the whole, in fact greater, though the difference has been declining and has been reversed in urban areas. Third, the patterns in rural and urban areas are fairly similar, with a slight tendency for the contribution of education to be higher in urban areas. The difference is in line with expectations, but its size is not, since in the more complex urban labour market it might be thought that education would have a much larger influence than in rural areas.

Table 2.5

Contribution of Education to Theil Index by Work Type and Sex (%)

		1983	*1993-94*	*2004-05*	*2011-12*
Rural regular	All	21	32	23	20
	Female	20	43	31	26
	Male	21	30	22	20
Rural casual	All	4	7	9	4
	Female	1	2	1	1
	Male	2	4	5	2
Urban regular	All	28	29	33	24
	Female	45	37	31	24
	Male	27	29	32	33
Urban casual	All	4	5	7	4
	Female	6	2	7	5
	Male	1	2	4	3

Of course, education affects not only the wage directly but also the likelihood of gaining access to regular work. The overall influence of education on wages is then a combination of the way educational credentials affect access to regular work and the influence on wages within each type of work. To analyse this further it is necessary to look at occupational differences, which we explore to a limited extent in Chapters 4 and 7.

2.5 Regional Inequality

As we saw in discussing the influence of social group, regional differences are important, and we need to consider regional inequality in more detail. There are substantial differences across India in levels of wages and incomes, which we need to take into account in our analysis. For this purpose we divide India into five regions. This was originally developed for comparisons with Brazil, where regional analysis has converged on a standard five-region breakdown. There is no comparable, consensual regional breakdown for India, so we have developed one specifically for this project. These regions consist of groups of states, on the basis of similarity in terms of output and expenditure per capita, poverty and urbanisation. These regions are the Northeast including West Bengal, Assam and nearby hill areas; a group of poor states in the Centre-North of the country; the Northwest, covering a rather heterogeneous group of states from Kashmir to Rajasthan, including Delhi; the South and West, a relatively more industrialised region extending from Gujarat to Tamil Nadu; and the state of Kerala, which is so different from the others that it is better to keep it apart.[5]

Figure 2.14 gives the ratios of mean wages, in rural and urban areas, between these different regions. The Centre, which is the poorest region in India, is considered as the reference point or the denominator of the wage ratio. These ratios are quite large in rural areas. The ratio was highest in Kerala in 1983 and has remained broadly constant over time. The Northwest also has a relatively high ratio, though it has been declining over time, and the same is true of the Northeast. The lowest ratio is observed in the south west, the industrial hub of India, where surprisingly rural wages are similar to those in the poor central region. The ratio however rose in 2012.

In urban areas, there is much less difference in wages across regions. The highest ratio was observed in all years in the Northwest,

5. The distribution of States by region is as follows: Northeast: West Bengal, Assam, other Northeast States; Centre: Bihar, Chhattisgarh, Jharkand, Madhya Pradesh, Odisha, Uttar Pradesh; Northwest: Delhi, Haryana, Himachal, Jammu/Kashmir, Punjab, Uttarakhand, Rajasthan; South and West: Gujarat, Maharashtra, Andhra Pradesh, Karnataka, Tamil Nadu; Kerala. More details are given in Barbosa et al. (forthcoming).

where it has been rising. All regions followed a different pattern. The north east saw a marginally declining wage ratio, the South and West's ratio remained fairly stagnant and quite low and in Kerala the wage ratio first fell and then recovered.

Figure 2.14

Regional Wage Ratios

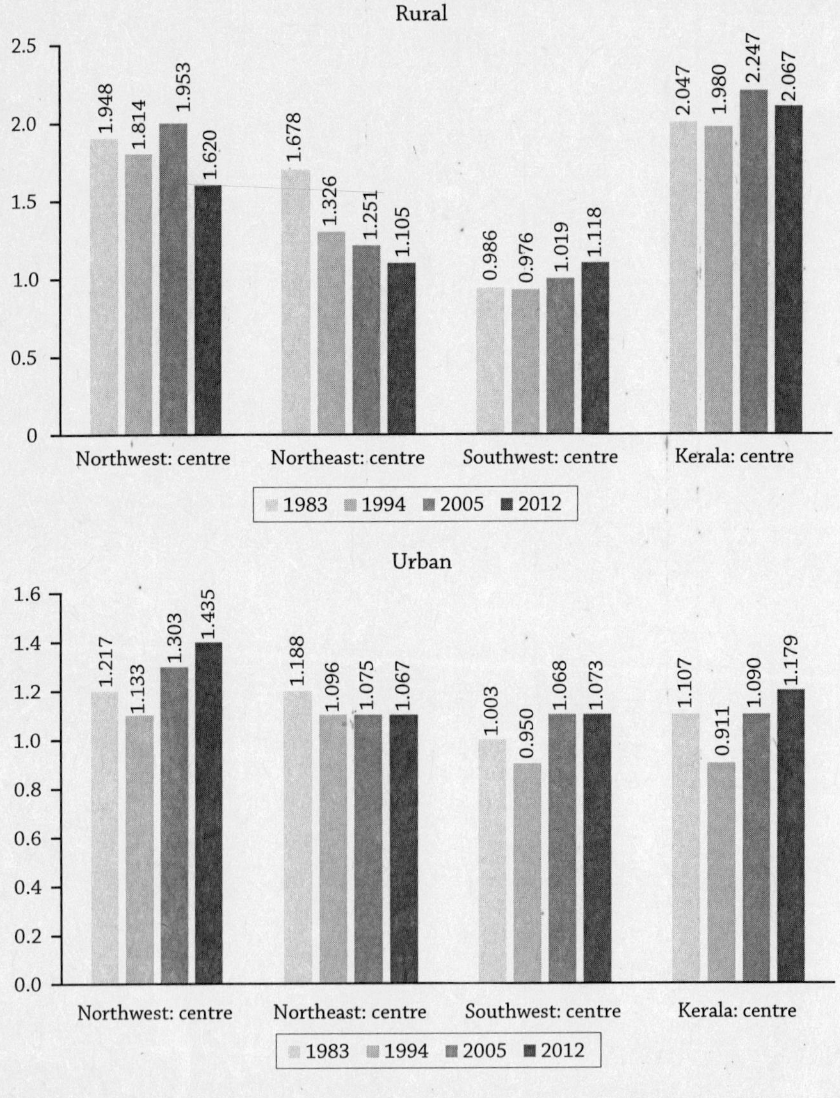

It can be argued from these patterns that the urban labour market is more integrated across the country than the rural labour market, and this is supported by the decomposition results in Figure 2.15. We see that the between-region component has contributed 4 to 5 per cent to overall regional inequality, without much change over time. However, the contribution is much greater in rural than in urban areas. In rural areas, regional differences accounted for between 9 and 10 per cent of inequality until 2011-12, when it dropped to 7. On the other hand, the regional contribution to urban inequality has been small, of the order of 1 per cent, but rising in 2011-12 when the rural contribution was falling.

Table 2.6

Contribution of Regional Differences to Theil Index by Work Type and Sex (%)

		1983	*1993-94*	*2004-05*	*2011-12*
Rural regular	All	4	1	4	5
	Female	7	3	5	5
	Male	4	1	4	6
Rural casual	All	14	24	28	24
	Female	18	18	22	11
	Male	11	25	31	30
Urban regular	All	1	0	1	2
	Female	4	3	3	4
	Male	1	0	1	2
Urban casual	All	7	10	18	14
	Female	12	8	13	9
	Male	6	10	23	18

It also appears that the regular labour market is more integrated across the country than the casual labour market, as can be seen from Table 2.6, which summarises a multilevel decomposition, and gives the contribution to the Theil index of regional differences broken down by regular and casual work, rural and urban and sex. It confirms the greater regional heterogeneity of the rural labour market, but also shows that regional differences contribute much less to wage inequality for regular than for casual work (24% in rural casual work in 2011-12 against 5% in rural regular; 14% in urban casual against 2% in urban regular). There is also a greater regional inequality in male than in female casual wages, and the gap seems to be growing over time. This is not true for urban regular wages, but the regional factor is much less important for this category.

Figure 2.15

Decomposition of Wage Inequality by Region: Overall, Rural and Urban

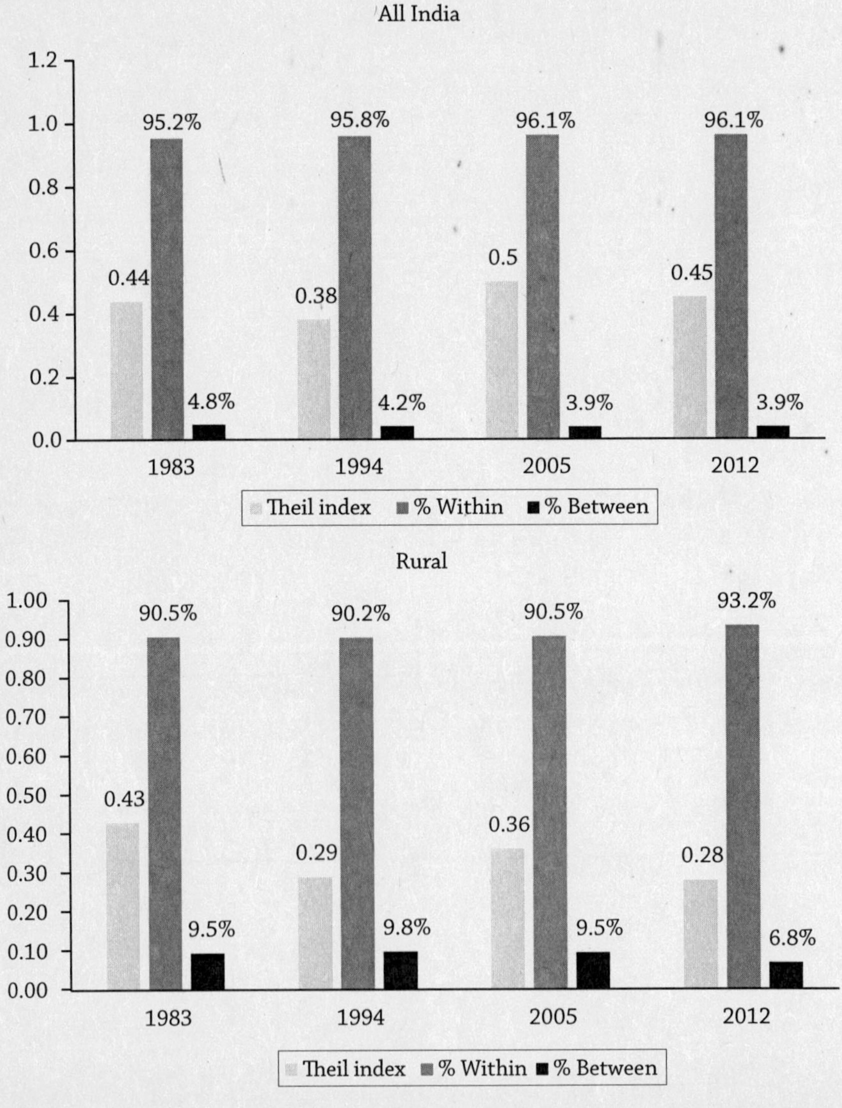

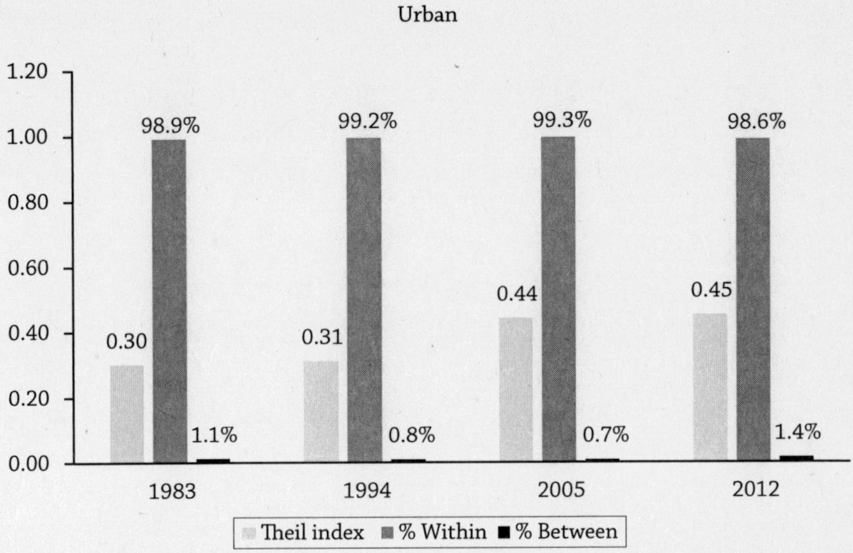

This suggests greater heterogeneity in rural areas than in urban, which seems quite plausible, and greater regional heterogeneity in casual labour markets than in regular, which is more of a surprise. The indication that regional inequality between urban areas has risen recently (Figure 2.15) also seems plausible, since the high growth of the Indian economy has not been evenly spread, although it is perhaps a surprise that the contribution of regional differences to urban inequality has been so small.

The experience of individual states shows that the time path of wage ratios between the state and the all-India average varies greatly from one part of the country to another (Figure 2.16). Tamil Nadu, Bihar, Punjab and Haryana all show a different pattern. In Haryana, the wage ratio has been high since 1983, initially falling and then rising since the 1990s. Haryana's neighbour, Punjab, shows precisely the opposite pattern, with wages in 2012 only 11 per cent above the national average. Wages in Bihar were low and have been falling further; while wages in Tamil Nadu, which were below the national average, have been close to the mean in the 2000s. The differences are such that we cannot interpret these outcomes as regional variations on a national pattern; the trends are so different that there are clearly distinct regional forces at work, and the trend at the national level may not be very meaningful. In reality while the decomposition above suggests that the contribution of regional to total inequality overall has not changed much, the regional composition of inequality has been changing substantially.

Figure 2.16

Wage Ratios, Selected States Compared with All India

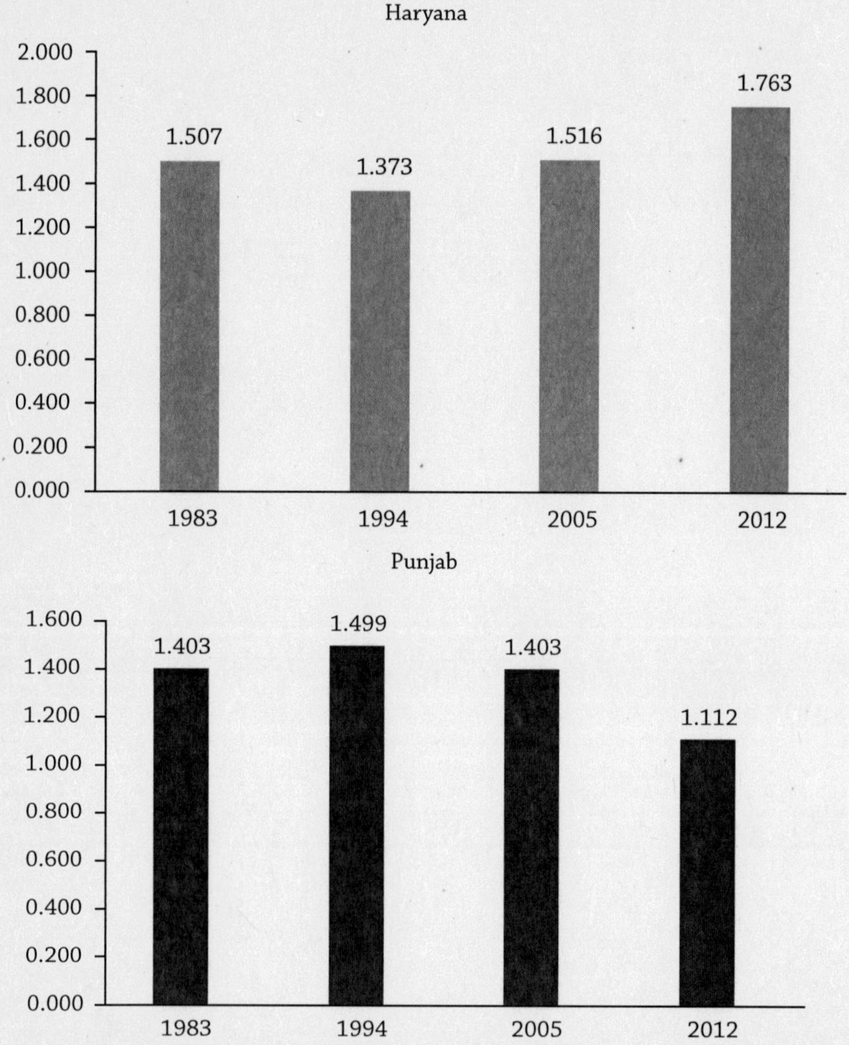

Bihar

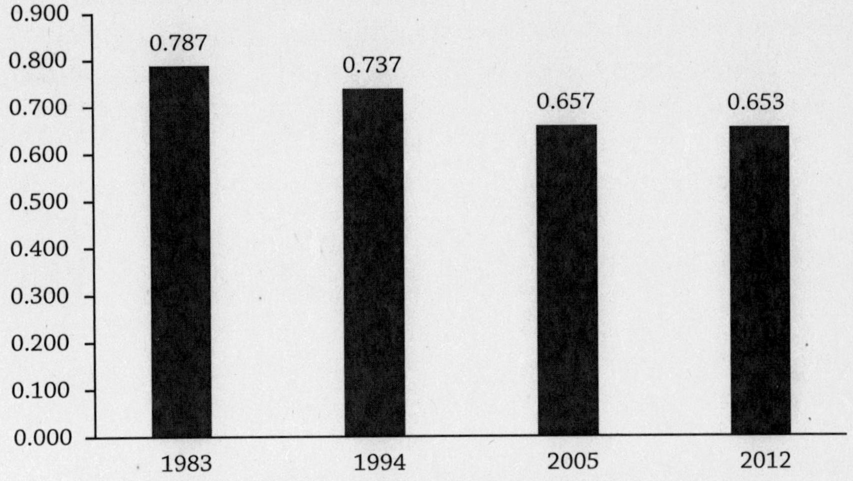

Tamil Nadu

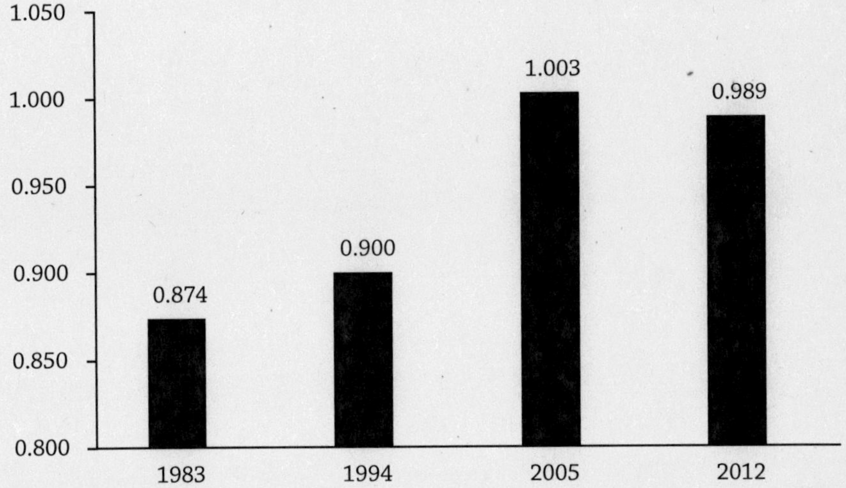

2.6 Summing Up

There are several insights to be retained from the above analysis, over and beyond the specific relationships identified.

First, the wage decompositions do not stand on their own as a guide to the importance of each of these factors in inequality. Each factor has not only a direct impact on wages, but also an indirect effect because of inequalities in access to work of different types. The declining contribution of gender to wage inequality has to be considered alongside the declining access of women to the labour market as a whole. There may not be much overt wage discrimination by caste or community, but caste and community networks are an important influence on employment opportunities.

Second, there can be distinct trajectories for different categories and groups, which may not appear in an overall analysis. This is very much clear for regional inequality, since there are large regional variations in development patterns, but it is also true for other groups. The increasing political influence of middle castes (OBCs) can change the nature and balance of caste inequality; or there may be particular educational qualifications which are important for access to higher paying jobs. Decomposition is a rather blunt instrument to analyse these mechanisms.

Third, there is a great deal of interaction between the five dimensions of inequality explored here. This can be seen in the selected multi-level decompositions presented above, but these only capture a part of the picture. We explore some multivariate relationships further in Chapter 4.

Appendix Table A.2.1

Theil Index Decompositions and Means

(i) Regular and Casual Wages: Theil Decomposition, Means and Ratios

	Year	*Theil Index*	*% Within*	*% Between*	*Mean Wages (current ₹)*		*Casual to Regular Wage Ratio*
					Regular	*Casual*	
Rural	1983	0.43	81%	19%	15.35	6.72	0.46
	1994	0.29	66%	34%	55.26	20.82	0.34
	2005	0.37	68%	32%	133.82	48.88	0.32
	2012	0.28	76%	24%	299.00	138.84	0.38
Urban	1983	0.30	82%	18%	23.11	9.51	0.40
	1994	0.31	78%	22%	75.81	28.73	0.36
	2005	0.44	86%	14%	193.68	69.39	0.36
	2012	0.45	88%	12%	450.37	171.48	0.37

Note: Wages in this section are in current prices.

(ii) Gender: Theil Decomposition and Mean Wages

	Year	*Theil Index*	*% Within*	*% Between*	*Mean Wages*					
					Male Regular	*Female Regular*	*Male Casual*	*Female Casual*	*Male All*	*Female All*
Rural	1983	0.43	92%	8%	15.98	11.16	7.76	4.78	10.20	5.46
	1994	0.29	89%	11%	58.75	34.57	23.68	15.58	31.32	17.07
	2005	0.37	92%	8%	144.94	85.54	55.15	34.64	78.81	42.67
	2012	0.28	95%	5%	322.39	201.46	149.70	103.25	192.97	123.15
Urban	1983	0.30	94%	6%	23.96	16.80	11.07	5.36	21.15	11.82
	1994	0.31	96%	4%	78.33	61.47	32.59	18.69	66.47	42.94
	2005	0.44	98%	2%	203.29	152.95	75.70	44.31	173.96	126.72
	2012	0.45	99%	1%	470.35	367.52	183.01	110.66	405.41	319.57

(iii) Socio-Religious Group: Theil Decomposition and Mean Wages

(a) SC/ST Compared with All Others

Sector	*Year*	*Theil Index*	*% Within*	*% Between*	*Mean Wages*	
					SC/ST	*Others*
Rural	1983	0.43	97%	3%	7.19	9.93
	1994	0.29	97%	3%	22.74	30.01
	2005	0.37	97%	3%	56.41	78.08
	2012	0.28	98%	2%	152.43	193.34
Urban	1983	0.30	97%	3%	14.27	20.87
	1994	0.31	97%	3%	45.24	65.95
	2005	0.44	97%	3%	118.89	177.72
	2012	0.45	98%	2%	291.80	416.84

(b) More Detailed Breakdown of Social Groups

	Year	*Theil Index*	*% Within*	*% Between*	*Mean Wages*						
					ST	*SC*	*Hindu OBC*	*Hindu Others*	*Muslim OBC*	*Muslim Others*	*Other Religion*
Rural	2005	0.37	92%	8%	48.78	57.97	66.11	107.62	77.24	66.51	90.61
	2012	0.28	94%	6%	130.69	155.68	175.35	251.04	170.53	178.00	228.14
Urban	2005	0.44	89%	11%	134.47	111.31	133.25	231.98	102.67	119.95	194.92
	2012	0.45	89%	11%	313.98	275.06	330.15	562.41	228.89	256.80	474.55

(iv) Education: Theil Decomposition and Mean Wages

	Year	Theil Index	% Within	% Between	Mean Wages: Not Literate	Literate without Formal Education or Below Primary	Pri-mary	Middle School	Secondary and Higher Secondary	Graduates and Above
Rural	1983	0.43	74%	26%	6.51	8.39	9.86	13.21	21.84	30.30
	1994	0.29	63%	37%	19.45	24.77	28.13	34.13	56.65	91.34
	2005	0.37	61%	39%	44.66	55.31	60.66	71.67	114.76	229.30
	2012	0.28	68%	32%	127.20	141.04	146.85	165.99	222.13	467.89
Urban	1983	0.30	66%	34%	10.47	14.26	14.64	17.92	26.24	39.05
	1994	0.31	62%	38%	31.14	39.54	41.03	49.63	75.43	121.72
	2005	0.44	61%	39%	67.49	84.24	90.41	103.29	168.71	326.22
	2012	0.45	63%	37%	162.96	184.63	193.28	221.08	330.86	721.36

(v) Region: Theil Decomposition and Mean Wages

	Year	Theil Index	% Within	% Between	Mean Wages: Northwest	Centre	Northeast	South & West	Kerala
Rural	1983	0.43	91%	9%	14.15	7.38	12.34	7.36	15.07
	1994	0.29	90%	10%	43.51	23.97	31.54	23.29	47.25
	2005	0.37	90%	10%	113.86	58.29	72.93	59.37	131.00
	2012	0.28	93%	7%	244.75	151.07	166.86	168.88	312.10
Urban	1983	0.30	99%	1%	22.42	18.64	22.19	18.84	20.56
	1994	0.31	99%	1%	70.22	62.29	68.61	58.87	56.15
	2005	0.44	99%	1%	196.64	150.93	162.31	161.18	164.51
	2012	0.45	99%	1%	507.19	353.46	377.20	379.24	416.70

3

Patterns of Inequality in Household Expenditure

The pattern of inequality of household expenditure may differ from that of wages for several reasons.

First, households are composites in which there are several different sources of income, which have a joint effect on overall household expenditure. Gender inequality, for instance, is less visible because men's and women's wage incomes are combined. Differences in incomes at different ages are also reduced insofar as different generations are present in the same household.

Second, there are additional sources of income beyond wage income. In particular, the National Sample Survey (NSS) employment survey does not record income from self-employment. Income from capital or land, and remittances, are also not taken into account.

Third, expenditure differs from income by the extent to which there is saving. In general, it is observed that saving is more unequally distributed, and expenditure more equally distributed than income.

Fourth, there is a question of household size to take into account. In this chapter, we use per capita household expenditure to adjust for household size. It should be noted, *en passant*, that a per capita adjustment is far from ideal if the aim is to measure equivalent levels of living across households of different sizes. Different household members have different needs and demands, and there are usually found to be some economies of household scale as well. However, this is the simplest and most widely used approach.

The first, third and fourth of these would tend to make the distribution of expenditure less unequal than that of wages. The second is a mix of factors which would have diverse effects, though income from capital would tend to be less equally distributed than labour income. But overall it is not surprising that, as we found in Chapter 1.1, the overall distribution of household expenditure per capita is distinctly less unequal than that of wages.

While some expenditure data are collected by the NSS as part of the employment survey, the more detailed expenditure data are from a separate expenditure survey using a different sample. We have preferred to use the latter, which appears to be more reliable, but this means that we cannot connect the detailed employment data with the expenditure data. Instead we use the more limited labour market information collected along with the expenditure survey. This permits us to break down households by (economic) type, based on the household's main income source (most frequently the occupation of the household head). The household types in urban areas are self-employed, regular wage/salary earning, casual labour and others. The last group presumably includes employers and rentier households. In rural areas we have self-employed outside agriculture, agricultural labour, other labour, self-employed in agriculture, and others. In 2011-12 we also can distinguish regular wage/salary work in rural areas. The household types are therefore different in rural and urban areas, though this is a reasonable reflection of the different economic systems.

Figure 3.1 shows the ratios of MPCE (mean per capita expenditure) across these groups in urban (since 1993-94) and rural (since 1983) areas.

In urban areas, self-employed households have expenditure which is well above casual labour households, the difference rising between 1993-94 and 2004-05 and then falling. But their expenditure is lower than regular wage households, with a gap that widens slightly over time. "Other" households do best, both in absolute terms, and in terms of the trend.

The ratio of expenditure in regular wage work households to that in casual labour households rises between 1993-94 and 2004-05 and then stabilises at just over double. This picture is slightly more favourable to regular wage work households than is suggested by the wage data.

Figure 3.1

Mean Per Capita Household Expenditure Ratios Between Household Types, Urban and Rural

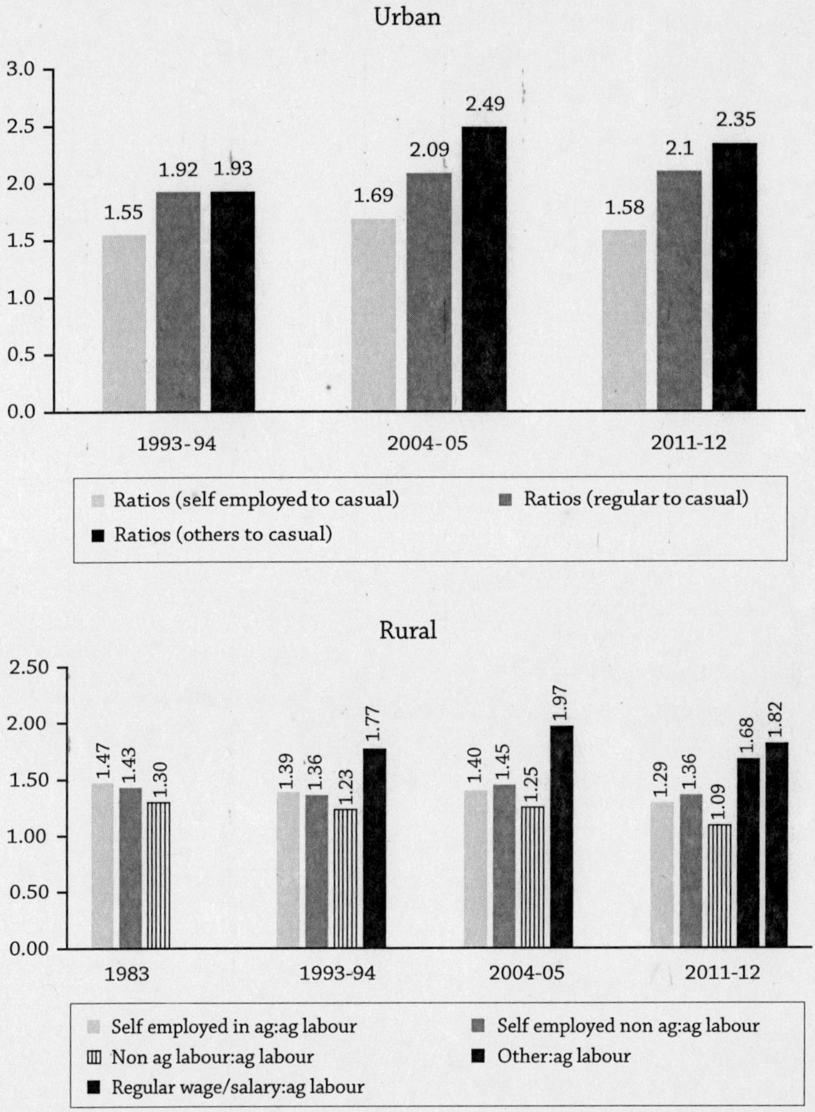

In rural areas, a more complex picture emerges. The self-employed, both in agriculture and non-agriculture, have expenditure per capita that is distinctly higher than agricultural labour households, but trending down, from a gap of 43 per cent to 47 per cent in 1983 to a gap of 29 per cent to 36 per cent in 2011-12. Non-agricultural labour too starts well above agricultural labour, but the gap is down to 9 per cent in 2011-12. However, in 2011-12 a part of this group may be classified into the regular wage work category, which shows expenditure much higher than agricultural labour; if we consider the two together there may not be much trend. The "other" group, including landlords and the economically inactive, has much higher expenditure though this declines after 2004-05.

Overall we see a tendency for the gaps between these categories to increase up to 2004-05 in urban areas, and then to stabilise or decline, consistent with our findings for inequality overall. In rural areas there is some tendency for casual agricultural labour to catch up with other groups. Again, the expenditure data are broadly in line with the wage data.

Figure 3.2 shows the decomposition of the Theil index of expenditure in terms of these household type categories. In rural areas, the between component rises from 6 per cent to 9 and then falls to 7 per cent; in urban areas it rises from 8 to 9 per cent. These figures are distinctly smaller than the contribution to wage inequality of the difference between casual and regular work. This may just reflect the tendency of household income to depend on a wider variety of factors. The changes over time are small and may not be significant.

A second classification of households that is available for expenditure per capita is by socio-religious group. A detailed breakdown is only available for 2004-05 and 2011-12. Figure 3.3 shows that in urban areas the groups that are clearly advantaged are Hindu "others" (basically upper castes) and other religions (i.e. other than Islam or Hinduism), both with expenditure about 80 per cent higher than SCs (scheduled castes) and STs (scheduled tribes). This gap shows some sign of declining between the two years. Muslims have relatively low expenditure per capita, especially OBC (other backward class) Muslims (OBC Hindus do better than the average).

Figure 3.2

Decomposition of the Theil Index of Inequality of MPCE Across Household Type, Urban and Rural

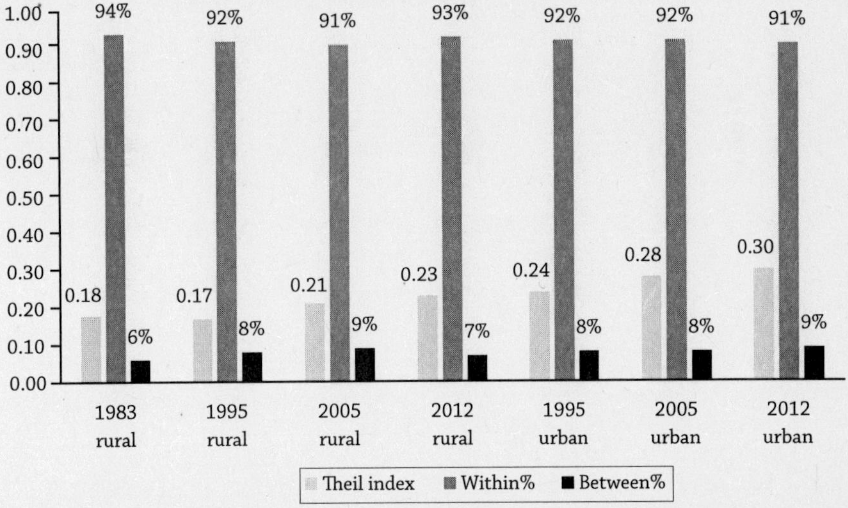

In rural areas the broad pattern is fairly similar, but there are a few significant differences. In particular, the relative position of STs is worse than in urban areas, while OBCs and Muslims do relatively better. The low expenditure levels of STs—distinctly lower than SCs—reflects their tendency to be concentrated in less developed rural areas of the country; in urban areas they do better, indeed slightly better than SCs. The same pattern was found for wages. In rural areas OBC Muslims have expenditure that is 20 to 40 per cent higher than STs, and 10 to 15 per cent higher than SCs; whereas in urban areas Muslims have the lowest expenditure level of all, even below SC and ST. The gaps mostly seem to be narrowing in rural areas, more so than in urban areas.

Figure 3.3

Ratios of Expenditure Per Capita Between Socio-religious Categories, Urban and Rural

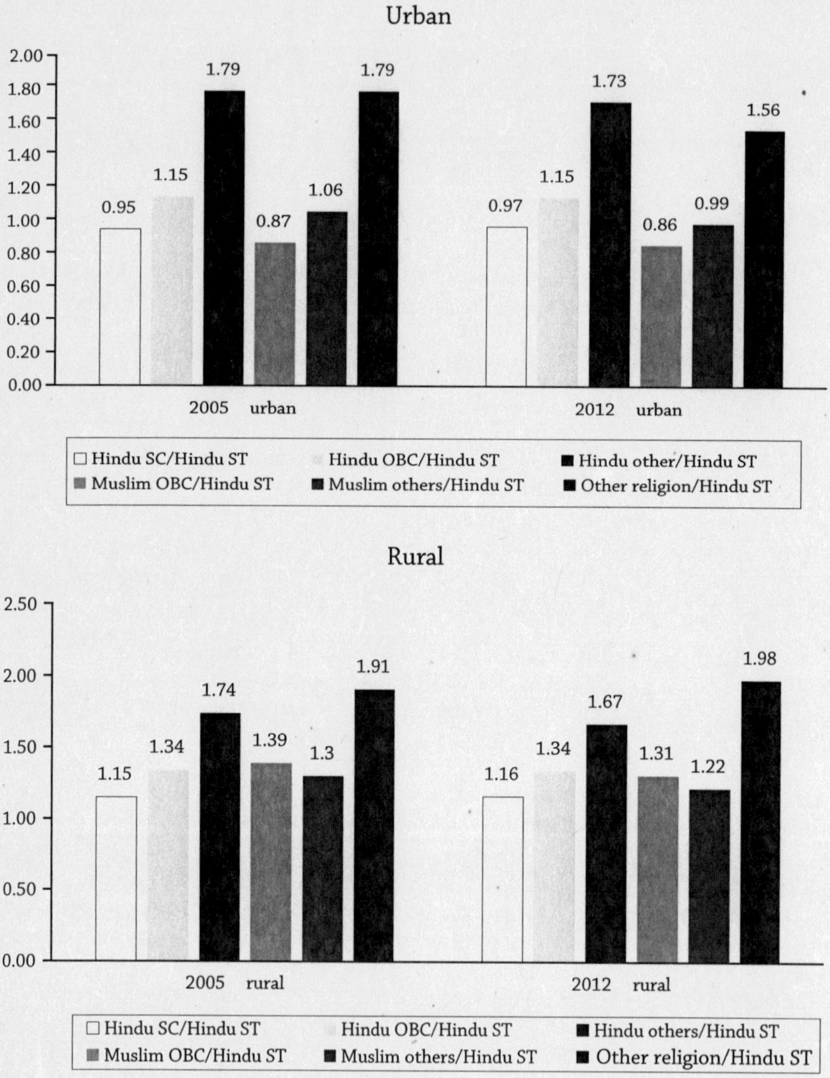

The decomposition of the Theil index for urban and rural combined (Figure 3.4, left-hand two bars) gives 12 per cent of inequality due to differences between these groups in 2004-05, coming down to 10 per cent in 2011-12. This is quite high—higher than the contribution of household economic type, for example. What is more, somewhat contrary to expectations, the figure is higher in urban than in rural areas (11% in the former in 2011-12 against 6% in the latter), although it has been declining in both. These patterns are quite similar to those for wages. It is clear that whatever the mechanism involved, social group continues to play a significant role in expenditure inequality.

Figure 3.4

Decomposition of Expenditure Per Capita by Socio-religious Group

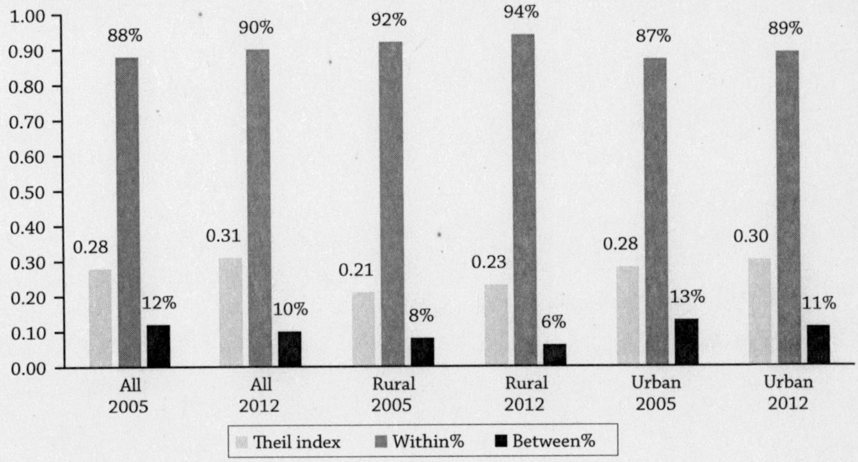

While the detailed breakdown is only available for 2005 and 2012, a more limited, and more conventional distinction, that between SCs and STs on the one hand, and all others, can be analysed over a longer period of time (Figures 3.5 and 3.6). In both urban and rural areas, the ratio of expenditure of others to expenditure of SC/ST peaked in 2004-05, with a difference of over 30 per cent in rural and over 40 per cent in urban areas; and then declined. But over the long term, since 1983, there has not been much change—a slight increase in urban areas, a slight decrease in rural. This stability does not suggest that policies in favour of SC and ST, which have been in operation throughout this period, are having much effect.

Figure 3.5

Ratios of Expenditure Per Capita Between Others and SC/ST, Urban and Rural

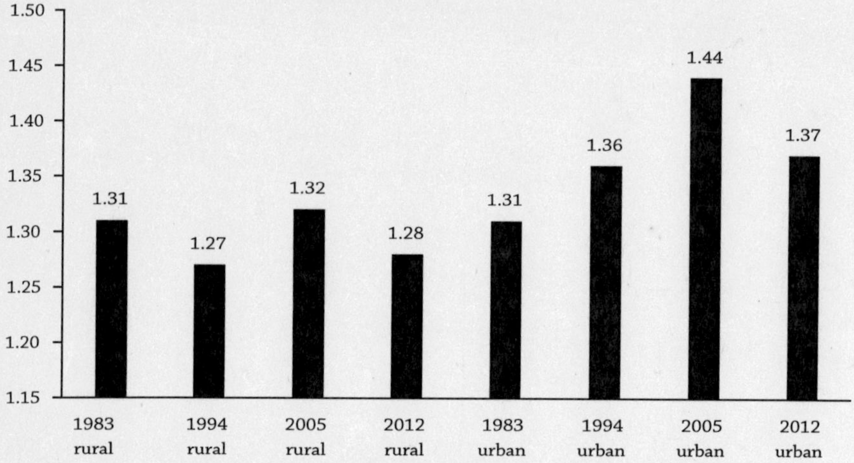

Figure 3.6

Decomposition of Expenditure Per Capita by Whether or Not SC/ST

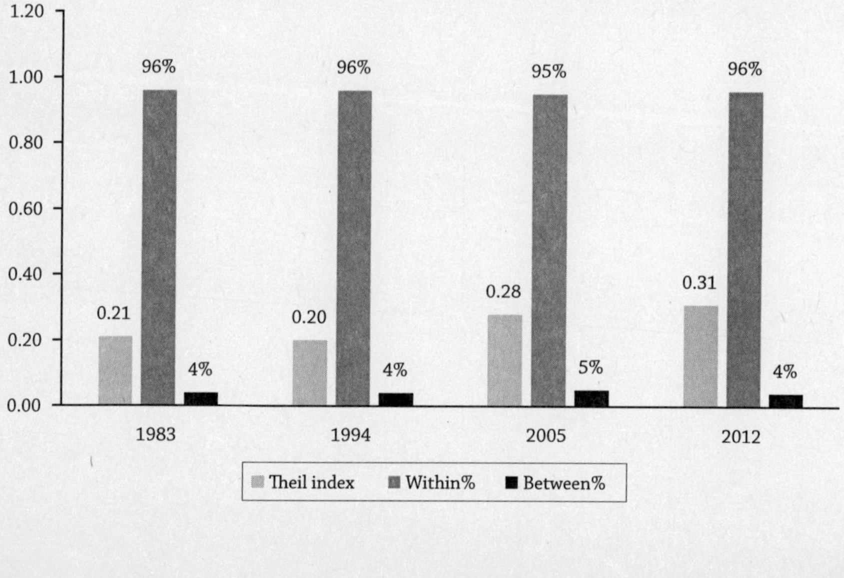

The decomposition results (Figure 3.6) suggest that the contribution to overall inequality is of the order of 4 per cent, and like the wage ratios is fairly stable over time. It is slightly higher in rural than in urban areas (not shown). So the difference between SC/ST and the rest accounts for some four tenths of the overall contribution of social group to expenditure inequality using the more detailed breakdown above.

Third we can decompose expenditure by the education of the household head (Figure 3.7). This, as expected, gives quite a strong relationship in urban areas, weaker in rural areas but still fairly substantial. In that respect the pattern is similar to that for wages, although the between component for expenditure is lower, especially in rural areas.

Fourthly, we break down by region (Figure 3.8), using the same five regions as for wages. In 1983, apart from the poorer Centre region, which lagged significantly behind, there was little difference between regions in average expenditure, with slightly more variation in rural than in urban areas. Over time, it can be seen that the regional differences grew. The Centre lagged further behind, the Northeast did only a little better, while the other regions gained, with the largest gains in Kerala. The general trend was similar in both urban and rural areas.

This is confirmed by the decomposition results (Figure 3.9). While the contribution of region to inequality was not large, it was larger in rural than in urban areas, and clearly rising in both, from 4 to 13 per cent in rural areas and from 2 to 4 per cent in urban areas. These results are somewhat different from those for wages. The greater contribution of region to inequality in rural than in urban areas is found in both, but in rural areas the wage decompositions gave some decline in the regional contribution after 2005, while the expenditure decomposition suggested a rise. The most likely explanation would lie in non-wage incomes—the implication is that in rural areas regional differences in non-wage incomes have increased faster than in wages in the most recent period. In urban areas, the regional contribution

Figure 3.7

Decomposition of Expenditure Per Capita by Education of Household Head, Rural and Urban

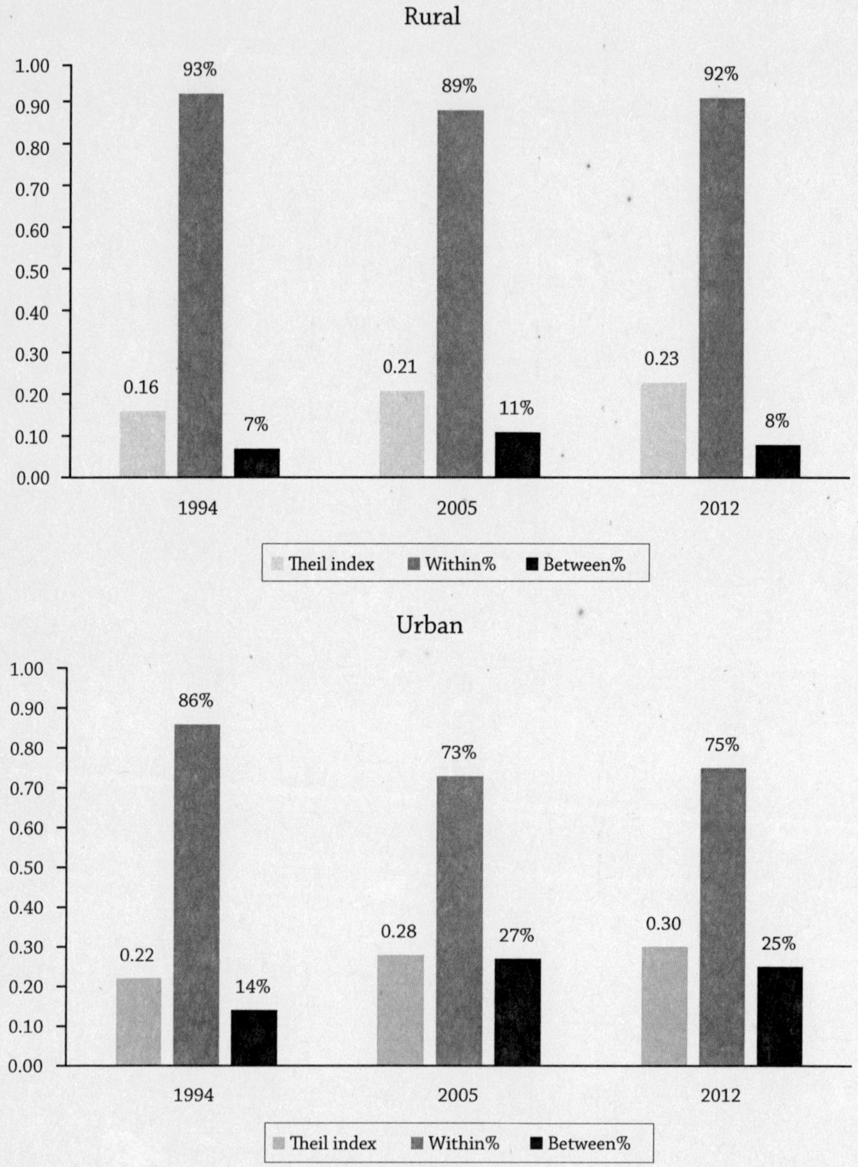

is somewhat higher than for wages than for expenditure, but the upward trend in the most recent period is found in both.

Figure 3.8

Ratios of Expenditure Per Capita Between Regions, Urban and Rural

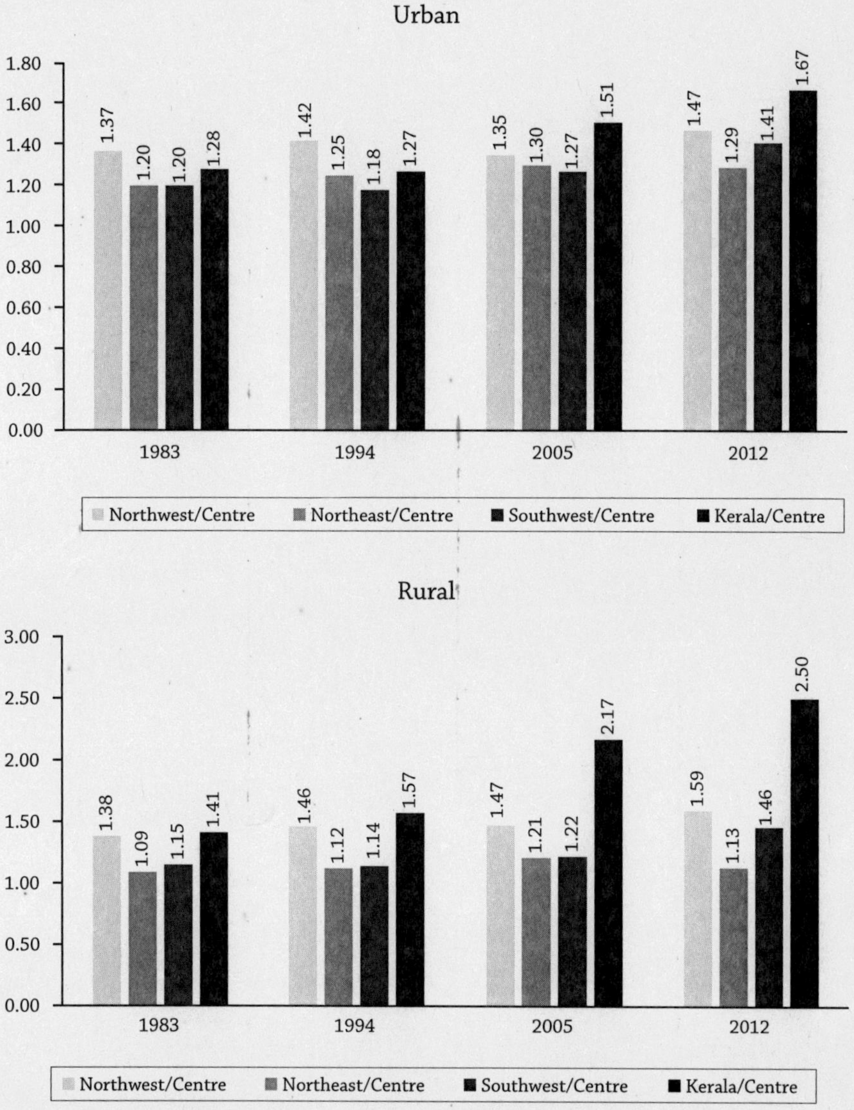

Figure 3.9

Decomposition of Expenditure by Region, Rural and Urban

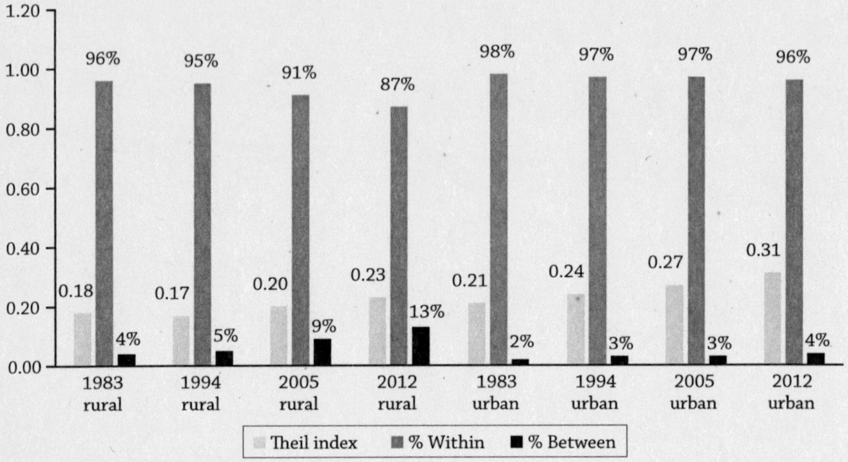

These three factors—household type, social group and region—interact, and a multilevel decomposition provides additional insights. Table 3.1 shows the contribution of social group to the Theil index within each of the household type categories. In urban areas there is a clear pattern, for the contribution is distinctly larger for the self-employed than for the wage employed, and also for regular workers

Table 3.1

Percentage of Theil Index of Expenditure Inequality Explained by Socio-religious Group within Household Type Categories, Rural and Urban (%)

		2004-05	*2011-12*
Rural	All	8	6
	Self-employed	7	6
	Labourers	4	4
	Others	6	4
Urban	All	14	11
	Self-employed	17	10
	Regular worker	10	8
	Casual worker	5	4
	Others	10	9

compared with casual workers among the wage employed. In other words, social group plays a significant role in the extent to which self-employment provides a decent income. Networks of contacts, and perhaps also access to capital, may be playing a role here. It also clearly differentiates better from less well-paid regular workers. Nevertheless, this pattern seems to weaken between the two dates in the survey, and is also distinctly weaker in rural areas (but in rural areas, self-employment mainly concerns cultivation, whereas in urban areas it covers a wide variety of occupations).

Like social group, education of the household head explains more of the variation in urban areas than rural (Table 3.2). Within urban areas, it contributes more to inequality among regular workers than among the self-employed in 2004-05, but in other respects the pattern is not greatly different from that observed for social group, with less contribution to inequality among casual than regular workers and a decline in the contribution over time. Education and social group, then, function in a rather similar way, reflecting, of course, the tendency for advantaged social groups to also have higher levels of education. In rural areas the pattern is less strong, with a larger contribution to inequality among the self-employed and the "other" group. This latter group (which also shows a fairly high figure in urban areas) includes employers, and presumably landlords and rentiers.

Table 3.2

Percentage of Theil Index Explained by Education of the Household Head within Household Type Categories, Rural and Urban (%)

		2004-05	*2011-12*
Rural	All	8	8
	Self-employed	5	7
	Labourers	2	4
	Others	8	13
Urban	All	25	17
	Self-employed	19	16
	Regular worker	24	14
	Casual worker	9	5
	Others	16	15

Unlike social group and education, region makes a much larger contribution to overall inequality in rural than in urban areas (Table 3.3). The largest contribution is found among labourers in rural areas and casual workers in urban areas. The small contribution to inequality among regular worker households in urban areas suggests a surprising homogeneity across regions.

Table 3.3

Percentage of Theil Index Explained by Region within Household Type Categories, Rural and Urban (%)

		2004-05	*2011-12*
Rural	All	9	13
	Self-employed	9	12
	Labourers	13	18
	Others	9	12
Urban	All	3	4
	Self-employed	5	7
	Regular worker	2	1
	Casual worker	7	12
	Others	10	6

To sum up these results for expenditure per capita, we can see some degree of consistency with the results of the wage analysis, notably with respect to decompositions by socio-religious category and education. For both of these breakdowns, the main features of the analysis of wages are reproduced in the analysis of expenditure. But for other variables there are some differences. The pattern of expenditure by household type cannot be directly compared with the nearest equivalent for wages, namely the distinction between casual and regular work. But it is noteworthy that the contribution of household type to expenditure inequality is much smaller than is the contribution to wage inequality of the distinction between casual or regular work. This is surprising since the number of categories is larger for household type. The trend over time is also weaker. The regional pattern too shows some differences between household expenditure per capita and individual wages, particularly in rural areas, where regional differences were narrowing in the wage data and widening in the expenditure data.

The most obvious source of these differences lies in the role of non-wage income, for which the pattern of inequality is no doubt different from that of wages—though we cannot observe that directly with NSS data. It is nevertheless interesting that the impact of education (of the head) and social group seem to be broadly similar for both wages and expenditure. However, there are a variety of other factors at play, including household composition, employment levels of different household members, the relationship between income and expenditure and other factors. So, it makes sense to analyse both wages and expenditure, which capture different dimensions of inequality.

The other point is that, as for wages, we really need a multivariate analysis to explore the relative importance of the different factors discussed above. We turn to that in the next Chapter.

Appendix Table A-3.1

(i) Household Type: Theil Decomposition and Mean Expenditure Per Capita

	Year	Theil Index	% Within	% Between	Mean Household Expenditure Per Capita					
					Self-employed in Agriculture	*Self-Employed in Non-agriculture*	*Regular Wage/ Salary Earning*	*Agricultural Labour*	*Non-agricultural Labour*	*Others*
Rural	1983	0.184	94%	6%	497	480		337	438	
	1993-94	0.171	92%	8%	503	492		362	444	640
	2004-05	0.206	91%	9%	583	604		416	520	818
	2011-12	0.228	93%	7%	715	754	1011	554	603	929
					Self-employed	*Regular Wage/Salary*	*Casual*	*Others*		
Urban	1993-94	0.239	92%	8%	862	1071	558	1079		
	2004-05	0.283	92%	8%	982	1213	580	1445		
	2011-12	0.304	91%	9%	1259	1671	796	1870		

Note: In 2004-05 prices. Other tables in this section give expenditure in current prices.

(ii) Socio-Religious Group: Theil Decomposition and Mean Expenditure Per Capita

	Year	Theil Index	% Within	% Between	Mean Household Expenditure Per Capita						
					ST	*SC*	*Hindu OBC*	*Hindu Others*	*Muslim OBC*		*Other Religion*
Rural	2005	0.21	92%	8%	408	469	548	709	567	532	778
	2012	0.23	94%	6%	951	1107	1276	1584	1246	1163	1885
Urban	2005	0.28	87%	13%	786	747	901	1404	687	832	1409
	2012	0.30	89%	11%	1871	1813	2145	3245	1606	1854	2926

(iii) Education: Theil Decomposition and Mean Expenditure Per Capita

	Year	Theil Index	% Within	% Between	*Mean Household Expenditure Per Capita*					
					Not Literate	Literate without Formal Education or Below Primary	Primary	Middle School	Secondary and Higher Secondary	Graduates and Above
Rural	1994	0.171	93%	7%	245	279	305	328	391	487
	2005	0.206	89%	11%	467	576	721	740	988	1291
	2012	0.228	92%	8%	1070	1171	1238	1412	1619	2104
Urban	1994	0.239	86%	14%	303	350	396	419	552	788
	2005	0.283	73%	27%	615	834	1133	1249	1774	2221
	2012	0.304	75%	25%	1427	1612	1773	1911	2465	4205

(iv) Region: Theil Decomposition and Mean Expenditure Per Capita

	Year	Theil Index	% Within	% Between	*Mean Household Expenditure Per Capita*				
					Northwest	Centre	Northeast	South & West	Kerala
Rural	1983	0.184	96%	4%	137	99	109	115	140
	1994	0.171	95%	5%	365	249	279	285	390
	2005	0.206	91%	9%	687	468	564	573	1013
	2012	0.228	87%	13%	1591	1003	1132	1469	2510
Urban	1983	0.215	98%	2%	190	139	167	167	179
	1994	0.239	97%	3%	555	390	485	461	494
	2005	0.283	97%	3%	1154	857	1111	1091	1291
	2012	0.304	96%	4%	2688	1831	2357	2587	3066

4

Multivariate Analysis

4.1. Multivariate Decomposition Using Fields' Method

This chapter combines all the categories we discussed in Chapters 2 and 3 into one unified multivariate analysis. The method used here is the Fields' decomposition (Fields 2002). In this method, a simple OLS (ordinary least squares) regression of log wages or log expenditure is conducted on various worker characteristics like age, education, social group, industry of work, etc. The coefficients obtained from this regression are used to calculate the share of each of these characteristics in the overall observed wage inequality.

For this decomposition we used the following characteristics of the individuals concerned for the wage analysis:

1. Age.
2. Rural-urban residence.
3. Sex.
4. Type of work (regular or casual).
5. Education (the six categories identified above).
6. Region (the five regions identified above).
7. Socio-religious group (the basic breakdown was as follows: SCs [scheduled castes], STs [scheduled tribes], Muslim, other. This was available for all four years. In 2004-05 and 2011-12 the more detailed categories identified above (pp.53-54) were also available.
8. Industry (standard 1-digit).
9. Occupation (standard 1-digit: note that the classification changed after 2005).

With the exception of the first, and of the last two, these are the variables which were used in Chapter 2. Age was added because it is generally included in earnings functions of this type as a proxy for experience; there is an expectation that productivity is a positive function of experience, so this should appear as a positive relation of wages with age. Industry and occupation were added because of the expectation that these are important influences on wages which need to be taken into account in a multivariate analysis.

We proceeded as follow. First, for each year, we proceeded stepwise, estimating several specifications:

1. The first included all the variables used in Chapter 2 (Spec.1)
2. The second added age (Spec.2)
3. The third added industry (Spec.3)
4. The fourth replaced industry with occupation (Spec.4)
5. The fifth included both industry and occupation (Spec.5)
6. For 2004-05 and 2011-12 we replaced the four category social group variable with the more detailed seven category variable (Spec.6).

These specifications were run first for all observations, with rural-urban an explanatory variable; and then for rural and urban areas separately.

Table 4.1

Fields Decomposition for Wages–Residuals (Unexplained Percentage) by Specification for 1983 and 2011-12

	Spec. 1	*Spec. 2*	*Spec. 3*	*Spec. 4*	*Spec. 5*	*Spec. 6*
			Overall			
1983	47.0	44.8	42.8	42.8	42.0	
2012	55.7	53.4	51.1	50.7	48.9	48.7
			Rural			
1983	59.5	57.9	55.5	55.3	54.3	
2012	67.9	66.7	63.7	64.7	62.7	62.3
			Urban			
1983	55.0	49.1	46.2	46.5	45.2	
2012	58.5	53.5	51.5	49.5	48.1	47.8

Table 4.1 gives the residuals—i.e. the unexplained portion—for each of these specifications for the first (1983) and last (2011-12) years. Several points can be noted:

1. First, the overall level of explanation is fairly high, between 32 and 58 per cent depending on the specification;
2. Second, the level of explanation is higher in urban areas than in rural;
3. Third, the more complete specifications did increase the level of explanation, especially in urban areas, but most of the explanation was delivered by the first specification;
4. Fourth, there was some increase in the residuals between 1983 and 2012, especially in rural areas.

We therefore observe that our model of wage inequality performs better in urban than in rural areas, and is also losing some explanatory power over time. But given that these are individual observations with random variation, errors and a variety of unobserved influences, the level of explanation can be considered fairly high.

Figures 4.1 to 4.3 present the results for all specifications for 2011-12, for all observations, and for rural and urban areas separately. The figure gives the percentage contribution of each variable to the decomposition, after excluding the residual.

In the first, basic specification in Figure 4.1, it can be seen that education accounts for more than half of the explanation, far more than any other factor. The rural-urban division, sex, work type and region all account for the order of 10 per cent, while social group (relsgroup) is negligible. Adding age in specification 2 improves the explanation to some extent but does not change this basic pattern. The addition of industry in specification 3 is largely at the expense of education, with only a small addition to the explanatory power. There is some interaction with work type, which is strengthened, and gender, which is weakened. However, when occupation is added instead of industry in specification 4, there is a substantial change. Occupation accounts for a quarter of explained inequality (as compared with 6 per cent for industry in the previous specification). Education remains the largest factor but is much weakened, as is work type (but of course occupation also to a large extent captures

Figure 4.1

Fields Decomposition of Wages, All Observations, Stepwise for 2011-12

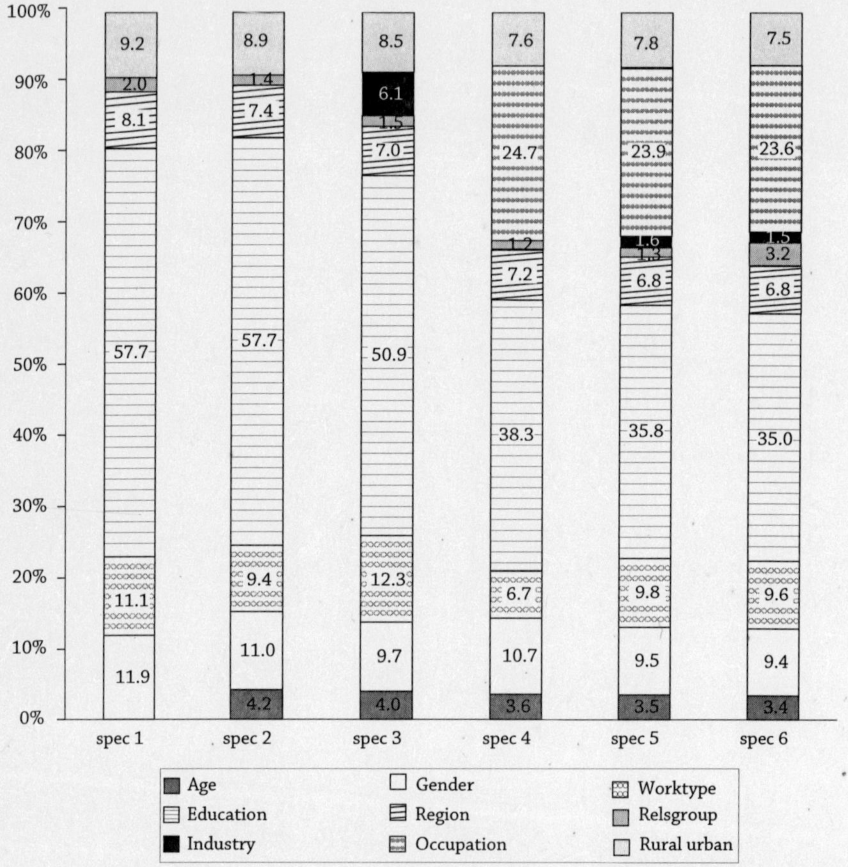

work type). There is little increase in explanatory power overall (Table 4.1). When occupation and industry are included together in specification 5, it is occupation that dominates, with little separate effect of industry. The final specification, 6, uses the more detailed breakdown for socio-religious group. It can be seen that this does increase the contribution of this variable (relsgroup), but its influence remains limited.

There are considerable differences between urban and rural patterns in Figures 4.2 and 4.3. Education is far more important in

Figure 4.2

Fields Decomposition of Wages, Rural, Stepwise for 2011-12

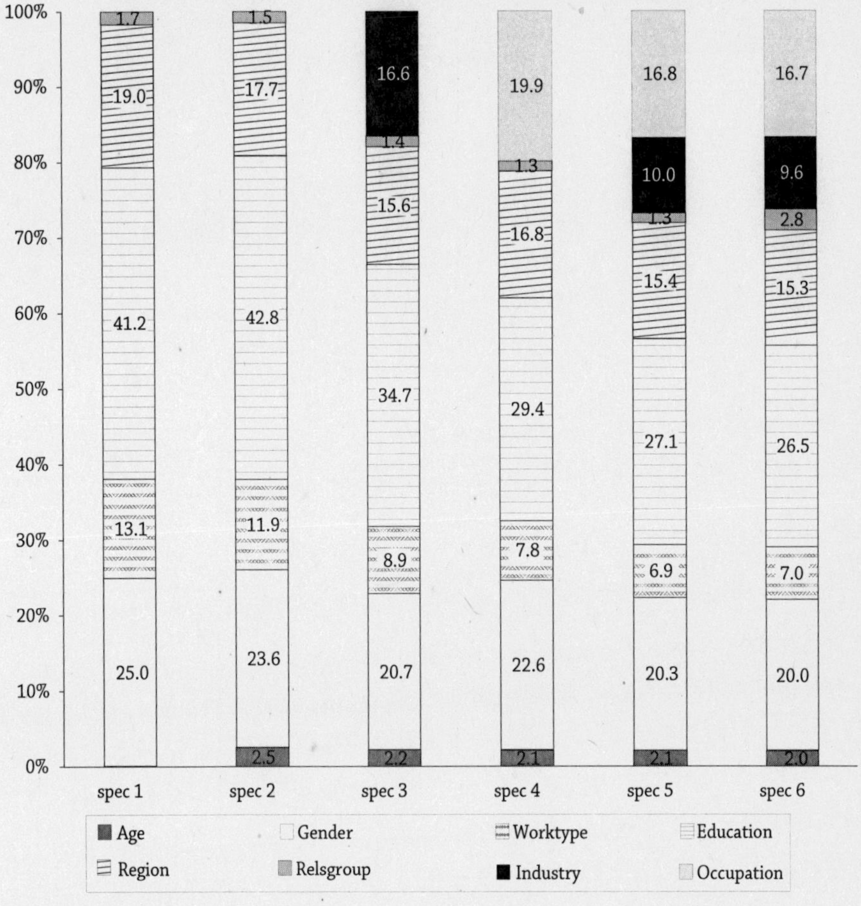

urban than in rural areas, but is weakened by the introduction of occupation (as is the case for the sample as a whole). In contrast, in rural areas industry plays a more significant role, though still less than occupation. The rural pattern clearly reflects the importance of the difference between agriculture and other sectors, whereas in urban areas, with a wider range of economic activities it is occupation that is more important than the industrial sector. Gender plays a more important role in rural than in urban areas, as does region, while age is more important in urban (no doubt reflecting the

Figure 4.3

Fields Decomposition of Wages, Urban, Stepwise for 2011-12

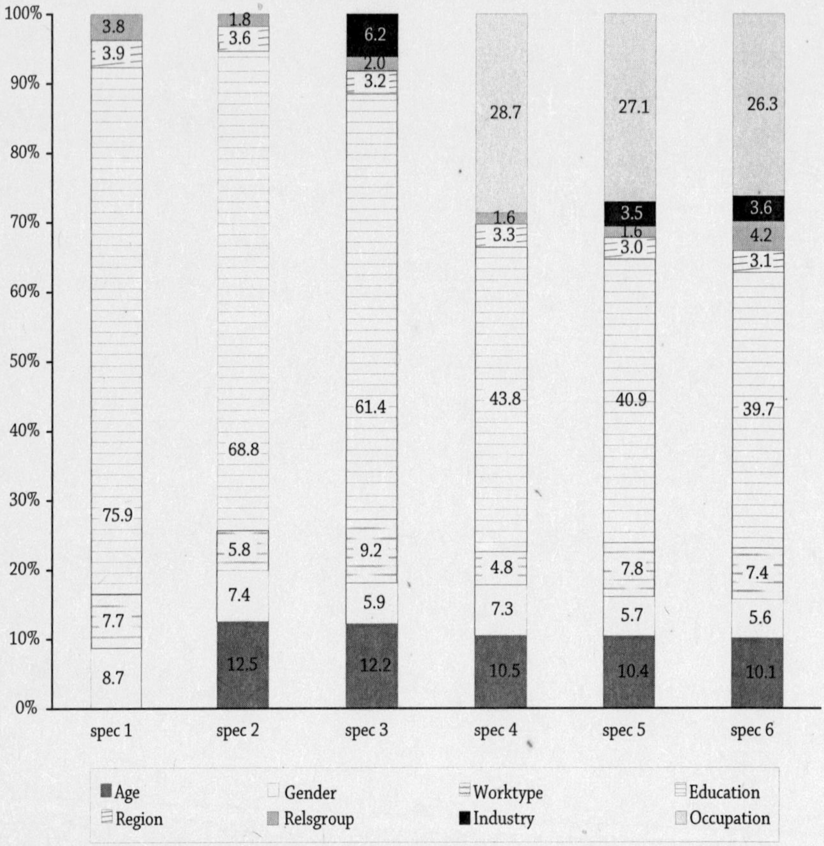

greater possibilities of career progression in urban areas). Work type is similar in the two cases while the influence of social group is small in both, though not negligible with the wider definition in specification 6.

How do we interpret these results? Education is the most important single factor. The fact that it is less influential in rural areas is a clear reflection of the relative lack of jobs in rural areas where educational qualifications are important. The relationship with occupation is also strong, but its interpretation is more ambiguous. It could be argued that education provides access to occupation, so the occupational variables may merely be a proxy for education. But occupation appears to have a significant influence independent of education, while there can also be common factors which provide access to both education and good occupations. The fact that occupation is much more important than industry (agriculture apart) is also an indication of the importance of this factor. Occupation should be considered jointly with the type of employment relation (casual/regular), which also contributes significantly in all specifications, in both rural and urban areas. In fact, if the sample is divided into regular and casual workers (detailed results not given here), we find that the decomposition of inequality is quite different within the two groups. That for regular workers is closer to the overall decomposition, while for casual workers regional differences are extremely important, but the role of education is small.

Among the other factors examined in Chapter 2, we see that gender inequality is important in all specifications, especially in rural areas, and is not much weakened by the introduction of industry and occupation—i.e., there is a gender effect independent of occupation and industry. Regional differences are significant too, especially in rural areas. Both of these results mirror the bivariate results. But the influence of socio-religious group is weaker, suggesting that much of the observed relationship with caste and religion is the result of social inequality with respect to education and type of work, rather than directly on wages.

Obviously, in the regression underlying the Fields decomposition, we are not considering the endogeneity of selection into the labour market as well as the opportunities and access (example, through social networks) that we do not observe but which influence wages. Differences in education levels or in labour market opportunities may be the result of caste or other hierarchies. In the next Chapter we undertake some preliminary analysis of the determinants of education with this point in mind.

The second way to look at these relationships is over time. Figures 4.4, 4.5 and 4.6 give the decomposition for 1983, 1993-94, 2005-06 and 2011-12. In each case we take the full specification (specification

5 rather than 6 because the detailed social group breakdown is not available for 1983 or 1993-94).

The overall decomposition in Figure 4.4 suggests that there have been some significant changes in the pattern of inequality over time, with some decline in the proportion of inequality explained by the model. First, it can be seen that the importance of occupation has increased, and that of industry has declined. It is certainly true that

Figure 4.4

Fields Decomposition of Wages, Overall, 1983 to 2011-12

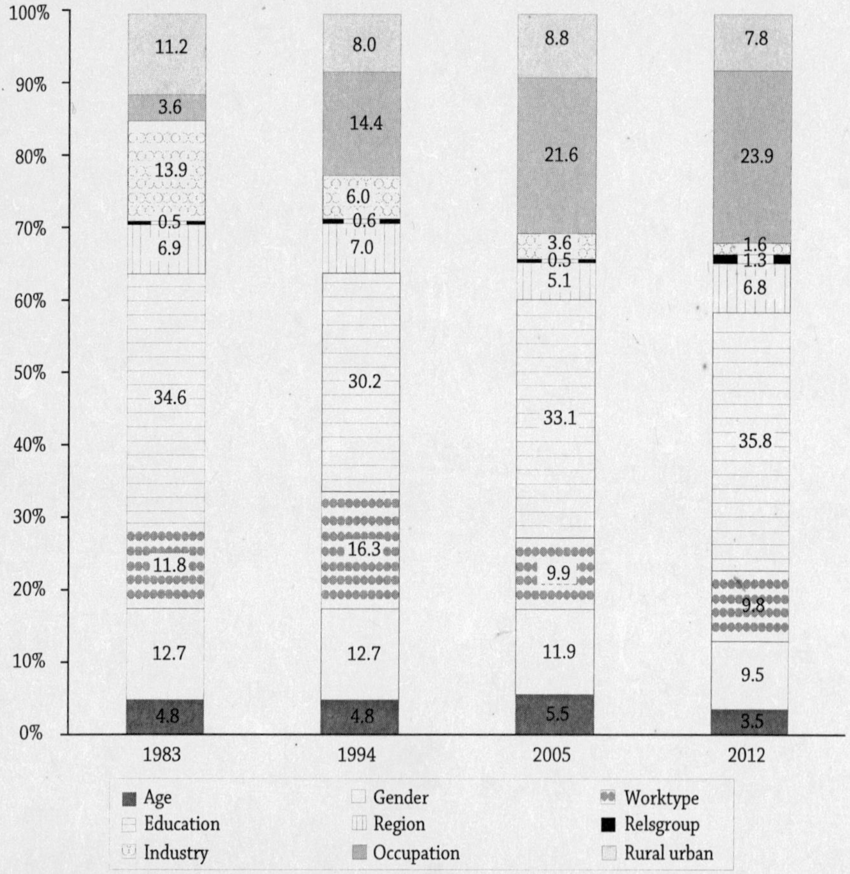

the Indian labour market has become much more complex over this 30 year period, including a much wider range of occupations. The decomposition suggests that this has been a major factor in the trend in inequality. It should be noted, that there was a change in the occupational classification in 2005, which may have influenced the results, but the increasing importance of occupation was visible prior to the change. If we combine occupation with work type (casual-regular) the total contribution to the decomposition has been relatively stable since 1993-94 at a little over 30 per cent, but with a shift away from the casual-regular breakdown towards a wider notion of occupation. The declining importance of industry as such suggests that inter-industry differentials have become less important after occupational structures are taken into account.

The other changes are smaller, but there are some clear trends. The importance of the rural-urban distinction has declined a little. The contribution of gender differences to overall inequality has also declined, which is in line with the bivariate results. Education shows little overall trend, while remaining the largest factor in each year.

These patterns are not identical in urban and rural areas. The urban pattern (Figure 4.6) is quite close to the overall pattern, with an increasing importance of occupation, a large and constant contribution from education, a declining contribution of work type and a sharply declining contribution of gender. Age is a significant factor too, but after rising up to 2005 it then declined. In rural areas, in contrast (Figure 4.5) the contribution of gender is large and rising, the upward trend in occupation is less consistent and industry also plays a role, work type first increases and then declines, while region is important throughout the period (negligible in urban areas). There is no clear trend in the contribution of education, which is distinctly lower than in urban areas throughout the period. Social group is not an important factor in either urban or rural areas, with the only sign of a trend in the slight strengthening in urban areas (but remaining small).

There are some important differences compared with the bivariate results. In rural areas, the multivariate analysis gives relatively greater importance to gender inequality (which is increasing rather

Figure 4.5

Fields Decomposition of Wages, Rural, 1983 to 2011-12

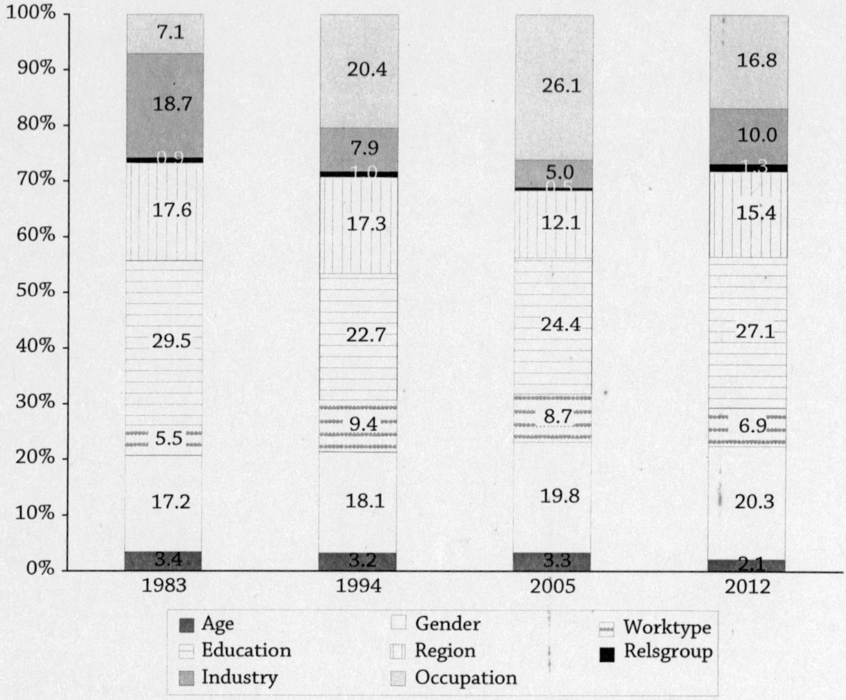

than decreasing), and also to region, as compared with education and work type. On the other hand, social group is as weak is in the bivariate analysis. In urban areas, again there is a greater importance given to gender inequality, but the multivariate analysis coincides with the bivariate in concluding that this impact is declining. The relative unimportance of region is confirmed, while social group does seem to be significant and of growing importance, but, as in the bivariate analysis, only with a more detailed breakdown including the OBCs. The preponderant influence of education in urban areas is confirmed, without any clear trend over the time.

It does seem that the impact of gender inequality comes out more clearly when other factors are also taken into account in the multivariate decomposition. For the impact of social group the

Figure 4.6

Fields Decomposition of Wages, Urban, 1983 to 2011-12

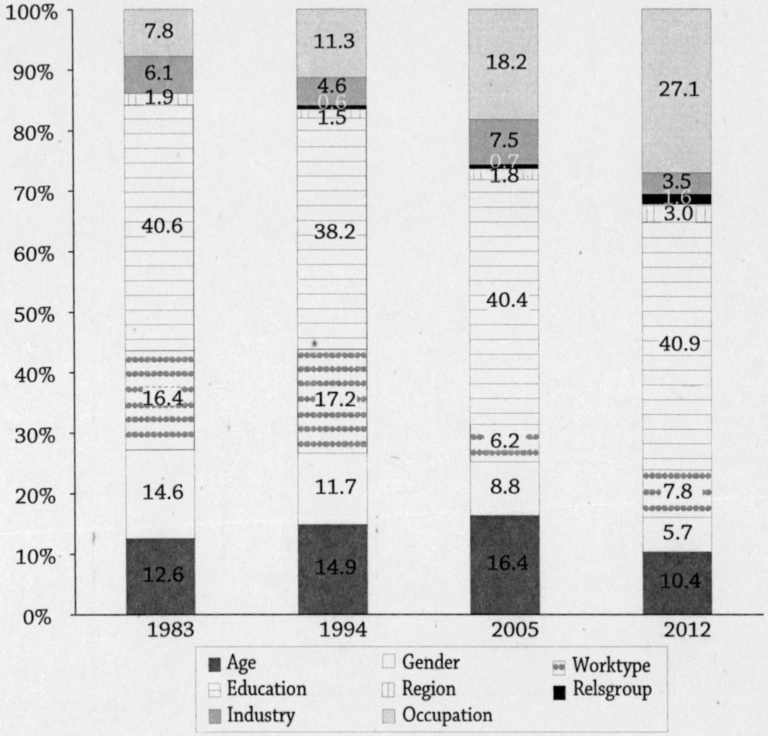

conclusion of the bivariate analysis stands, that there are so many local factors that an all-India analysis may miss the key relationships, so no strong conclusion should be drawn—except that the overall impact is weaker than one would expect from the political rhetoric.

We also estimated the Fields decomposition for household expenditure per capita, although since there are less explanatory variables available, and they are characteristics of the household rather than of individuals, this is a more limited exercise which cannot be compared directly with the results for wages. We included the following independent variables:

1. Rural-urban residence.
2. Household type (in the categories discussed in Chapter 3).

3. Education of the household held (the six categories identified above).
4. Region (the five regions identified above).
5. Socio-religious group (the more detailed categories identified in Chapter 3).
6. Industry (standard 1-digit) of the household head.
7. Occupation (standard 1-digit) of the household head.

We have consistent information on household economic type only for 2004-05 and 2011-12 and report only for those two years. All decompositions were done separately for rural and urban areas.

Table 4.2

Fields Decomposition for Household Expenditure Per Capita, Residuals by Specification for 2004-05 and 2011-12

	Spec. 1	*Spec. 2*	*Spec. 3*
	Rural		
2004-05	73.2	72.6	72.7
2011-12	71.4	71.5	71.3
	Urban		
2004-05	60.4	59.9	60.0
2011-12	61.9	61.2	61.0

Three specifications are reported: the first included the core variables: household type, education, region and socio-religious group. The second added industry of the head, and the third replaced industry by occupation. Table 4.2 gives the residuals for each of these specifications for the two years in the two areas. It can be seen that: (a) the level of explanation for expenditure was lower than for wages (i.e. the residuals are higher); and (b) there was very little gained by adding industry or occupation to the decomposition. Nevertheless, in Figures 4.7 and 4.8 we give the decompositions for these three specifications in 2011-12. It can be seen that in neither urban nor rural areas do industry or occupation make a substantial contribution to the model, nor do they have much effect on the other variables, slightly reducing the impact of household type in both regions, and

Figure 4.7

Fields Decomposition of Per Capita Household Expenditure, Rural, Stepwise for 2011-12

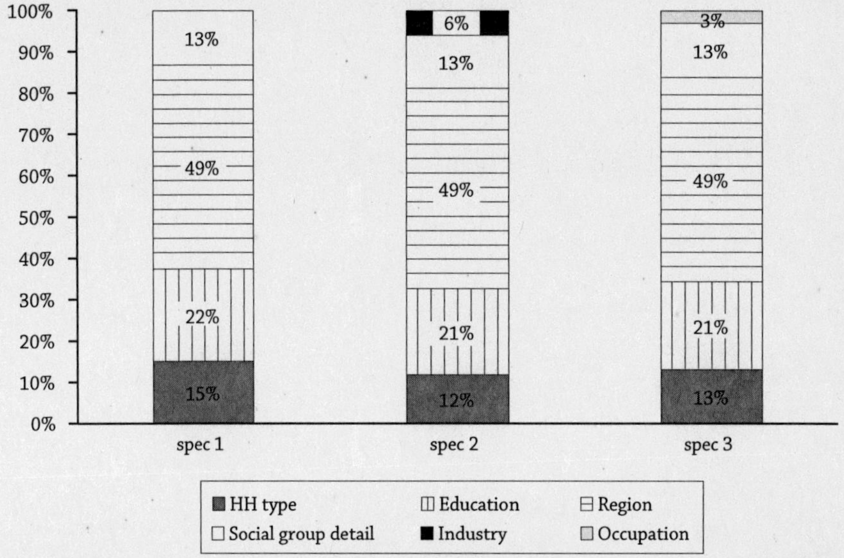

Figure 4.8

Fields Decomposition of Per Capita Household Expenditure, Urban, Stepwise for 2011-12

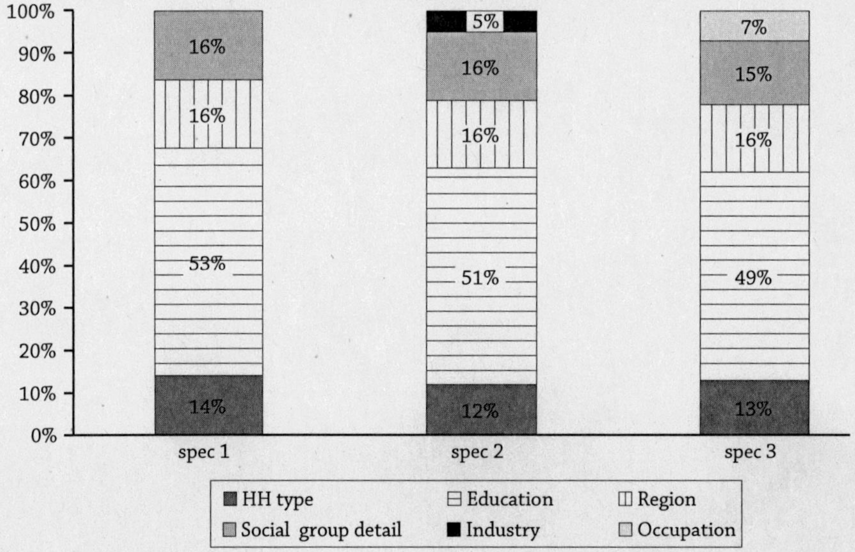

the impact of education in urban areas. In reality, the household type variable captures the essential occupational differences between households.

In the light of the above results we only analyse the basic specification (Figure 4.9). In rural areas, we see that the most important factor is region, which increases substantially between the two years. Next in size is education, which declines slightly, followed by household type, declining sharply, and social group, which declines slightly. The reasons for these trends are not clear, though they are not inconsistent with the bivariate results. It should be noted that the residual for rural areas is over 70 per cent, so our confidence in the model is less than that for wages.

In urban areas the results also show an increase in the importance of region, though here the education of the household head dominates the results, the changes are less sharp and the residuals are smaller at around 60 per cent.

One interesting result is that socio-religious group is much more important for the expenditure decomposition than for wages, with the other major difference being the greater importance of regional differences. In both cases it is plausible that non-wage income would be an important reason for these differences.

Figure 4.9

Fields Decomposition of Per Capita Household Expenditure, Rural and Urban, 2004-05 and 2011-12

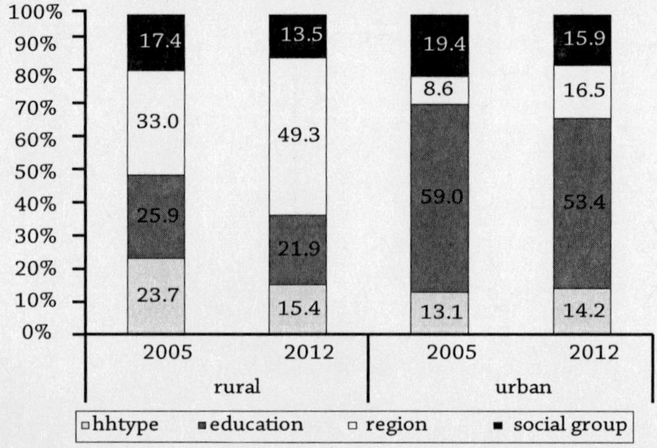

4.2. Multivariate Analysis of Education

In the decompositions of wages, the most important factor is usually education, a result that is very common in this type of analysis. But this may be misleading, since the underlying assumption of independence among the explanatory variables does not hold. In reality, education is itself the outcome of a process of social differentiation. In particular, caste, sex, region, household income and wealth, education of the head and a number of other factors are important determinants of the educational levels attained by family members. When wage differentials are attributed to education, in reality they often have their roots in these social differentials. Standard economic theory would attribute wage differentials across education levels to productivity differentials due to investment in human capital. This effect is certainly present, but at the same time differentials in the labour market reproduce the prevailing social hierarchies, and the relative importance of productivity and structural inequality is not easy to ascertain.

We cannot solve this problem here, but we can at least explore how far education levels are associated with some of these more structural factors. Tables 4.3 and 4.4 give the results of a set of Probit estimates in which the dependent variable is alternately whether individuals have education: (1) below and above college and (2) below and above secondary and higher secondary school, restricted to ages 20 to 29, for urban and rural areas respectively. This selection is made because differentiation is now occurring mainly in the upper echelons of the education system, and the age group 20 to 29 gives an indication of what was happening in the 10 to 15 years before the date of the survey (since the education of older adults reflects previous periods). The independent variables are socio-religious category (either limited to the identification of ST and SC, before 2005, or the more detailed breakdown used above, for the most recent two years); sex; and region. In rural areas land ownership is also available. These estimates use the NSS employment surveys.

Table 4.3

Probit Estimates: Dependent Variable, Education Level of Population Aged 20 to 29, Urban

	(1)	(2)	(3)	(4)	(5)	(6)	(7)	(8)
Dependent Variables	*College Education or Above (Value 1) or Not (Value 0)*				*Secondary Education or Above (Value 1) or Not (Value 0)*			
	1983	*1994*	*2005*	*2012*	*1983*	*1994*	*2005*	*2012*
Non ST/SC (base: ST/SC)	0.743***	0.658***			0.687***	0.660***		
	(0.00125)	(0.000941)			(0.000780)	(0.000645)		
Socio-Religious Group (Excluded Group: ST)								
Hindu SC			-0.158***	-0.0435***			-0.166***	0.0148***
			(0.00170)	(0.00122)			(0.00137)	(0.00106)
Hindu OBC			0.186***	0.311***			0.169***	0.372***
			(0.00161)	(0.00115)			(0.00131)	(0.00101)
Hindu Other Caste			0.711***	0.675***			0.832***	0.814***
			(0.00159)	(0.00115)			(0.00131)	(0.00103)
Muslim–OBC			-0.428***	-0.325***			-0.363***	-0.260***
			(0.00195)	(0.00132)			(0.00152)	(0.00112)
Muslim–Non OBC			-0.0108***	-0.240***			-0.0271***	-0.108***
			(0.00173)	(0.00131)			(0.00140)	(0.00112)
Other Religion			0.691***	0.623***			0.752***	0.787***
			(0.00179)	(0.00134)			(0.00154)	(0.00128)
Female (Base: male)	-0.238***	-0.0721***	-0.0515***	-0.0838***	-0.364***	-0.309***	-0.164***	-0.0980***
	(0.000637)	(0.000531)	(0.000434)	(0.000361)	(0.000490)	(0.000433)	(0.000389)	(0.000347)

Region (Base: Northwest)								
Centre	-0.00763***	-0.0332***	0.139***	-0.0679***	-0.0998***	-0.123***	0.0542***	-0.124***
	(0.000981)	(0.000842)	(0.000742)	(0.000629)	(0.000794)	(0.000717)	(0.000664)	(0.000605)
Northeast + WB	-0.0916***	-0.136***	-0.144***	-0.181***	-0.0318***	-0.137***	-0.119***	-0.275***
	(0.00123)	(0.00107)	(0.000922)	(0.000811)	(0.000967)	(0.000892)	(0.000807)	(0.000772)
Southwest	-0.223***	-0.241***	0.116***	0.0338***	-0.0961***	-0.144***	0.127***	0.105***
	(0.000904)	(0.000777)	(0.000674)	(0.000564)	(0.000711)	(0.000651)	(0.000600)	(0.000552)
Kerala	-0.260***	-0.373***	0.394***	0.308***	-0.273***	-0.136***	0.397***	0.441***
	(0.00219)	(0.00172)	(0.00141)	(0.00130)	(0.00167)	(0.00131)	(0.00130)	(0.00134)
Constant	-1.684***	-1.469***	-1.168***	-0.810***	-0.799***	-0.488***	-0.319***	-0.00608***
	(0.00139)	(0.00110)	(0.00166)	(0.00122)	(0.000923)	(0.000807)	(0.00136)	(0.00109)
Pseudo R-squared	0.0338	0.0252	0.0624	0.0556	0.0378	0.0341	0.0797	0.0709

Notes: Standard errors in parentheses. *** $p<0.01$, ** $p<0.05$, * $p<0.1$

Table 4.4

Probit Estimates: Dependent Variable, Education Level of Population Aged 20 to 29, Rural

	(1)	(2)	(3)	(4)
Dependent Variables	*College Education or Above (Value 1) or Not (Value 0)*		*Secondary Education or Above (Value 1) or Not (Value 0)*	
	2005	*2012*	*2005*	*2012*
Socio-Religion (Base: ST)				
Hindu SC	0.289***	0.389***	0.346***	0.359***
	(0.00111)	(0.000884)	(0.000666)	(0.000530)
Hindu OBC	0.442***	0.549***	0.562***	0.602***
	(0.00101)	(0.000803)	(0.000602)	(0.000477)
Hindu Other Caste	0.815***	0.971***	1.023***	1.134***
	(0.00103)	(0.000829)	(0.000633)	(0.000526)
Muslim–OBC	0.0934***	0.0588***	0.153***	0.161***
	(0.00158)	(0.00120)	(0.000986)	(0.000718)
Muslim–Non OBC	0.229***	0.458***	0.355***	0.554***
	(0.00143)	(0.00114)	(0.000830)	(0.000709)
Other Religion	0.649***	0.825***	0.703***	0.904***
	(0.00135)	(0.00116)	(0.000899)	(0.000843)
Female (Base: male)	-0.363***	-0.264***	-0.492***	-0.418***
	(0.000434)	(0.000355)	(0.000288)	(0.000255)
Regions (Base: Northwest)				
Center	-0.0746***	-0.315***	-0.128***	-0.182***
	(0.000724)	(0.000554)	(0.000490)	(0.000425)
Northeast + WB	-0.268***	-0.382***	-0.195***	-0.205***
	(0.000960)	(0.000739)	(0.000611)	(0.000535)
Southwest	0.0889***	-0.0657***	0.0995***	0.184***
	(0.000732)	(0.000565)	(0.000502)	(0.000443)
Kerala	0.813***	0.702***	0.810***	0.894***
	(0.00106)	(0.000952)	(0.000837)	(0.000847)
Ln landowned pc	0.0514***	0.0580***	0.0734***	0.0766***
	(9.97e-05)	(8.21e-05)	(6.65e-05)	(5.81e-05)
Constant	-2.123***	-1.839***	-1.344***	-0.987***
	(0.00122)	(0.000949)	(0.000765)	(0.000622)
Pseudo R-squared	0.0819	0.0861	0.1002	0.1058

Notes: Standard errors in parentheses. *** $p<0.01$, ** $p<0.05$, * $p<0.1$

Without discussing these results in detail here, since that is not the main focus of this monograph, it can be seen that there are powerful effects of caste, sex, religion and region. In both urban (Table 4.3) and rural (Table 4.4) areas, the probability of obtaining these higher levels of education is much higher for upper (Hindu) castes and religions other than Islam and Hinduism, with Scheduled Castes, Scheduled Tribes and Muslims disadvantaged to differing degrees in rural and urban areas. Women have a much lower probability than men of higher education levels in both areas, and there are also strong regional effects, with Kerala well ahead, and the Northeast and the rural Centre well behind. In rural areas land owned per capita was also highly significant (no comparable variable was available for urban areas).[1]

This strongly supports the thesis that education levels are endogenous. This implies that the effects of education observed in the multivariate decomposition are an overestimate of its direct impact. In reality, a more complex model is required which captures the structural determinants of inequalities in education as well as inequalities in wages or expenditure, and it cannot be assumed that the observed direct relationship between education and wages or expenditure will be reproduced if there is an exogenous change in education due to state policy.

1. Since education levels are attained prior to the date of the survey, and may influence household income or wages, we have a problem of simultaneity if we use the latter variables in these estimates. This can also be to some extent true of wealth, but wealth (especially land ownership) is much more stable over time and less influenced by current educational levels.

5

Relationship Between Income and Expenditure Inequality

In India, the measurement of inequality at the household level most frequently relies on expenditure data, usually from the National Sample Survey (NSS). Income would be a better measure for many purposes, but there is no regular national survey that collects income data.

Since, this monograph is intended to be used for a comparison of inequality in India and Brazil, this is a problem. In Brazil, the measurement of inequality most frequently relies on income data, often from the PNAD (National Household Sample Survey). There is an expenditure survey, but it is less frequent, and the PNAD survey is needed to link household income with the labour market data.

This difficulty does not apply to wage data. A broadly comparable analysis of wage inequality is possible in the two countries, along the lines of that above. But it is also desirable to examine income inequality at the household level. Household income reflects the patterns of employment and wages of all household members, income from own business or self-employment, returns on capital, land and other assets and public and private transfers. In Brazil we can aggregate different income sources within the household to calculate total household income. We cannot do this in India using the NSS, which provides only an estimate of household expenditure, along with some components of household income (notably wages, but not self-employment incomes or capital incomes).

So to compare household level inequality in India and Brazil we usually find ourselves comparing income data with expenditure data. What biases does this introduce?

A first answer to this question can be given by comparing the distribution of household income and household expenditure distribution within India. The Indian Human Development Survey carried out by the National Council of Applied Economic Research (NCAER) in 2004-05, the same year as the 61st round of the National Sample Survey (NSS), collected both income and expenditure data, and has been used along with the NSS to make this comparison. We calculate Gini and Theil indices for wages (NSS), for household expenditure (both NSS and NCAER surveys), and for household income (NCAER). Figure 5.1 gives the results.

It can be seen that:

1. The Gini and Theil indices are quite consistent with each other in terms of the patterns for the different variables.
2. Expenditure inequality as measured in the NCAER survey is similar to, but slightly higher than in the NSS survey.
3. Income inequality, as measured by the NCAER survey, is much higher than expenditure inequality: a Gini of about 0.54 for income, against 0.37 (NSS) or 0.40 (NCAER) for expenditure. In fact, the Gini coefficient of income inequality in 2004-05 is not much different from the corresponding figure for Brazil, although the latter country is usually regarded as much more unequal.
4. Inequality of wages is also higher than inequality of expenditure (in the NSS survey).
5. Inequality of wages in the NSS data is almost as high as inequality of income in the NCAER survey (the difference is larger for the Theil index than for the Gini coefficient). We would normally expect the distribution of wages to be less unequal than the distribution of income, since non-wage income is, on the whole, less equally distributed than wage income, so this is in line with expectations. However the difference is quite small.

Figure 5.1

Theil Index and Gini Index Compared Between Surveys and Across Different Variables, 2004-05

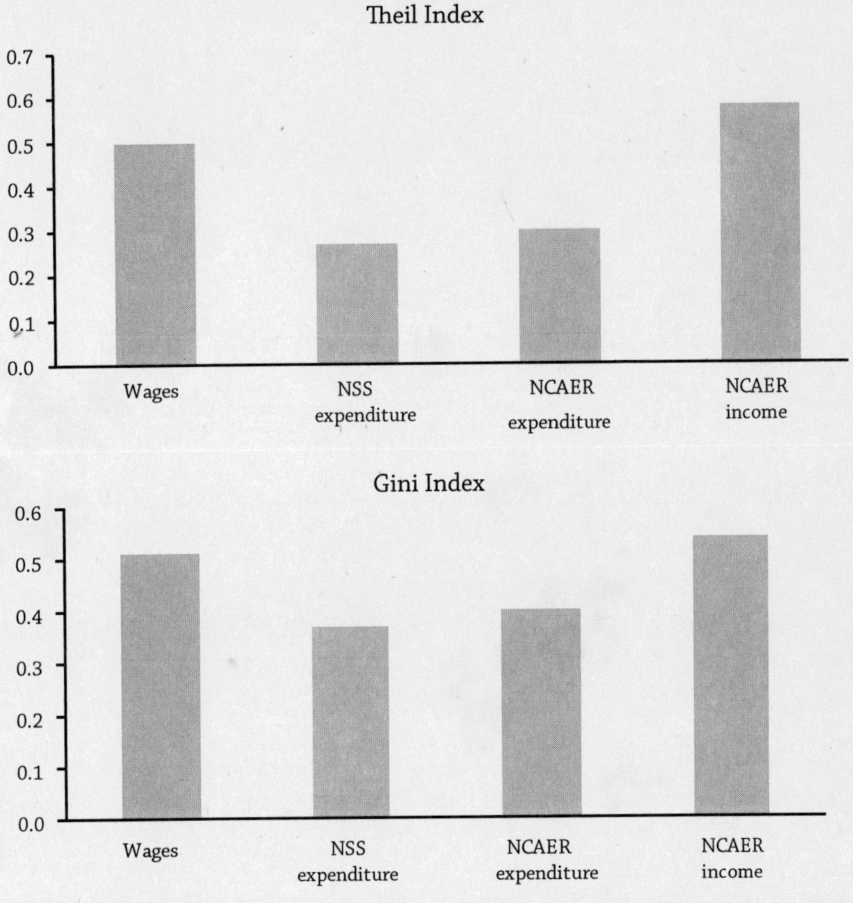

Sources: NSS 61st round unit level data (left hand two bars) and NCAER Human Development Survey 2004-05 (right hand two bars)

These results confirm that the different measures of inequality do not give identical results. As we saw in chapter 1, the trends can also be different; the trend of inequality in wages was fairly similar to that in expenditure in urban areas, but there were significant differences in rural areas, with inequality of expenditure rising in the most recent period (after 2004-05) when inequality of wages was falling.

Since a second NCAER survey has been carried out in 2011-12, it will be possible in due course to explore whether changes over time in the inequality of income and of expenditure are similar. The 2011-12 data were not available at the time of writing this monograph.

6

The Functional Distribution of Income

In India, the functional distribution of income is heavily influenced by two important aspects of economic structure. The first is the share of the 'unorganised' sector in GDP. The unorganised sector, according to the conventional Indian definition, comprises all small and household enterprises (small being less than 10 workers with electrical power, and less than 20 without). In 1980-81, the unorganised sector accounted for 68 per cent of GDP. Even in 2007-08 it accounted for 57 per cent. A part of reason of this lies in the importance of agriculture in GDP, which accounted for 38 per cent in 1980, although it was down to 16 per cent in 2010. The second is the importance of self-employment, which accounted for 58 per cent of all employment in 1983, and was still 52 per cent in 2011-12. These two facts are closely related, since self-employment occurs mainly in the unorganised sector, and a majority of employment in the unorganised sector consists of self-employment. Of course, much self-employment is in agriculture, which has declined, but the decline in work in agriculture is much greater than the decline in self-employment, so some self-employment in agriculture has clearly been substituted by self-employment in other sectors (mainly tertiary).

The importance of this lies in the fact that returns to labour and returns to capital (or land) are very difficult to separate for the self-employed. In the national accounts, the conventional way to handle this is through the category of mixed income, i.e. income which is a mix of returns to labour, capital and land. Figure 6.1 shows that over the period from 1980 to 2008, the share of mixed income declined fairly steadily, from over 54 per cent to less than 44 per cent, with a period of relative stability between 1986-87 and 1993-94. This decline of 11 percentage points corresponds fairly close to the similar decline in the share of the unorganised sector in GDP.[1]

Of the remaining components of factor shares, wages were fairly stable around 38 per cent up to 1991-92. They then declined unevenly to 34 per cent in 2007-08. But the large change was in the profit share, which rose from 8 per cent in 1980-81 to 22 per cent in 2007-08. Most of this increase occurred in the period after liberalisation in 1991-92.

Since much mixed income derives from self-employment, a substantial proportion of mixed income represents returns to labour. So a good part of the decline in mixed income certainly corresponds to a decline in returns to labour. So these overall figures show a substantial shift in factor incomes away from labour to capital.

This can be seen more clearly when we look at the organised sector alone (Figure 6.2), which does not record mixed income in the national accounts. Over the period from 1980-81 to 2007-08 the wage share declined from 74 per cent to 48 per cent, with the bulk of the decline again occurring after 1992-93. This did not occur in the unorganised sector (not shown), where the share of wages rose slightly from 20 to 24 per cent, with a corresponding decline in mixed income. This, no doubt, reflects a decline in the share of agriculture within the unorganised sector, and may be due to formerly self-employed small farmers moving into wage work in the urban unorganised sector.

The mechanisms by which this occurred can be seen in more detail for the manufacturing sector, for which the Annual Survey of Industry (ASI) provides data (Figure 6.3). The profit share in manufacturing industry was fairly stable in the 1990s at around 20 per cent. After 1992-93 it rose to a plateau of around 30 per cent before rising sharply to between 50 and 60 per cent in the 2000s. Meanwhile, the share of wages to workers, over 30 per cent in the 1980s, dropped steadily after 1990 to not much more than 10 per cent. ASI data distinguishes payments to workers from 'emoluments'

1. Due to a change of definitions in the national accounts we cannot extend this analysis beyond 2008.

Figure 6.1

Factor Shares, Whole Economy, India, 1980-81 to 2007-08

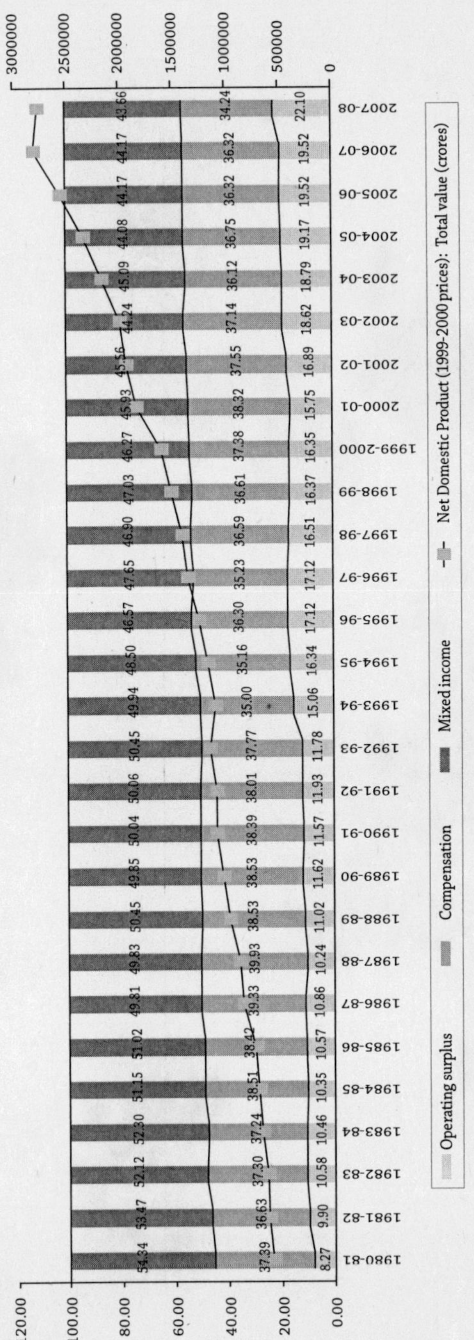

Source: National Accounts

Figure 6.2

Factor Shares, Organised Sector, India, 1980-81 to 2007-08

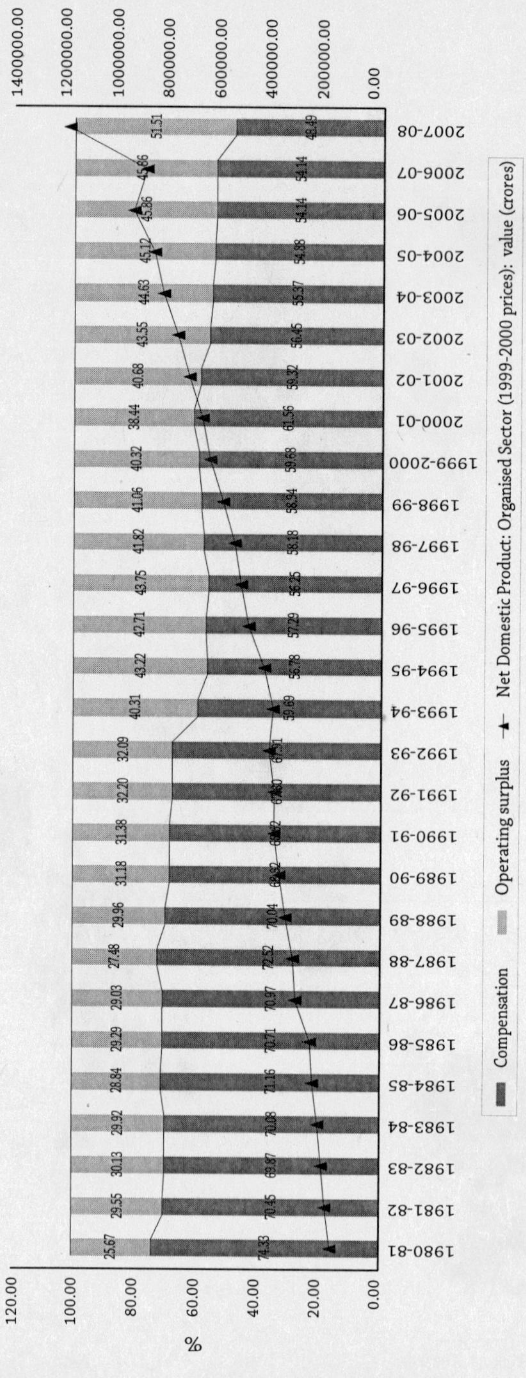

Source: National Accounts.

to technical, managerial and professional staff. This too declined, but much less sharply than payments to workers, from 20 to 25 per cent in the 1980s to just under 20 per cent in the 2000s. There was also a shift from rental and interest payments to profits after 2002-03, which appears to reflect the increased ability of organised sector firms to generate capital internally.

Figure 6.3

Factor Shares in the Organised Manufacturing Sector, 1981-82 to 2011-12

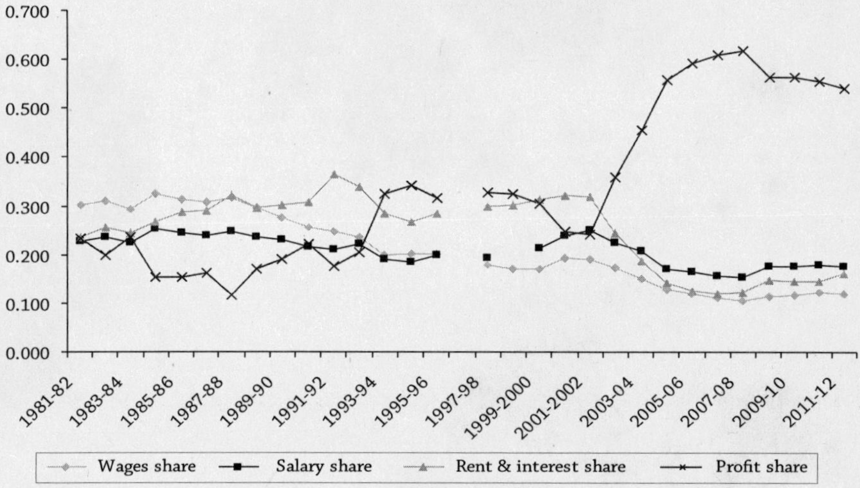

Source: Annual Survey of Industry.

Apart from the decline in rent and interest, the increase in the profit share derived from two principal factors. The first was a relatively slow rise in total (organised sector) employment compared with the growth in output (Figure 6.4). It was this that led to concerns in India about 'jobless growth'. The second was a relatively slow rise in daily wages and salaries (Figure 6.5). Indeed, for wage workers there was little increase at all. Real wages of workers in organised manufacturing rose up to the beginning of the 1990s, but thereafter showed little change until the mid 2000s. Wages (salaries) of technical and professional workers, on the other, after flattening out in the 1990s, rose steadily thereafter, so the ratio between them and unskilled workers doubled, from twice in the 1980s to four times around 2010. There was therefore an increasing differentiation among the manufacturing workforce. After 2005, however, both wages and salaries started to rise, and the gap between them stabilised.

Figure 6.4

Employment (Millions) and Output (₹ Trillion in 1999-2000 Prices) in Organised Manufacturing, 1981-82 to 2011-12

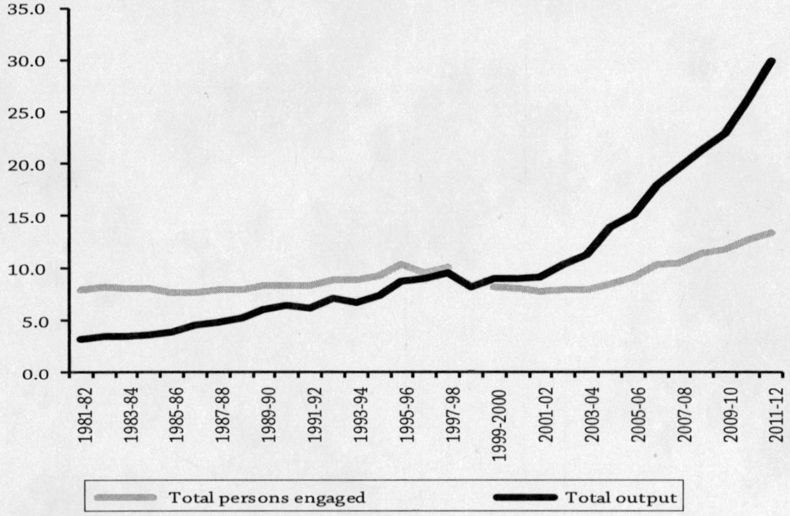

Source: Annual Survey of Industry.

The main shift in factor incomes away from wages and towards profits occurred in the wake of the economic liberalisation of the early 1990s. But the dynamics were clearly complex, with an initial rise in the profit share occurring during a period when there was little change in wages (but rising incomes for professional and technical workers); and a further rise in the profit share after 2005 which was partly at the expense of rent and interest, and only partly at the expense of wages, which started to rise significantly in real terms as the growth of the economy accelerated.

Figure 6.5

Real Wages in Organised Manufacturing, Waged and Salaried Workers (₹/day in 1999-2000 Prices), 1981-82 to 2011-12

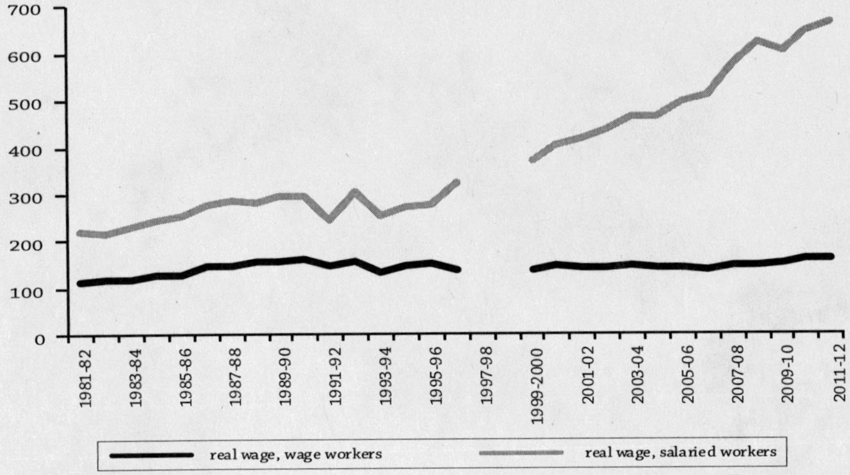

Source: Annual Survey of Industry.

7

Occupation and Inequality

Patterns of Access and Remuneration

As we have seen in the multivariate decompositions (chapter 4), occupational differences account for a substantial fraction of wage inequality. Most of this monograph has focused on wages, but occupational inequality is important not only because different occupations pay different wages, but also because occupations vary greatly in their intrinsic interest, stability and social valuation.

There are three main aspects to this issue: the pattern of access to different occupations; changes in occupational patterns over time; and occupational differences in wages and incomes.

7.1 Access

There are considerable differences in occupational opportunity between men and women, between different social groups, and between other population categories. These can in part be traced to skills and qualifications, in part to the functioning of networks of patronage and control, and in part to various forms of discrimination.

Mamgain (2016) has compiled occupational data from the same four National Sample Survey (NSS) rounds that we have used in this monograph.[1] This shows that compared with men, a higher proportion of women are found in agricultural occupations and personal services (Table 7.1). Women are less well represented than men among white collar and executive positions, and among production workers. Over time, women have improved their position

1. It should be noted that the occupational classification changed in 2005, so that a complex and in some respects imperfect mapping exercise is required to align occupational categories after 2005 with occupational categories before that date. This is discussed in Mamgain (2016).

compared with men in professional and technical occupations, and to some degree in clerical occupations. However, this refers to the share of these occupations among working women, and—as we saw in Chapter 2—the proportion of women in economic activity is much lower than that of men and showing some tendency to decline.

Table 7.1

Occupational Pattern by Sex, 1983 and 2011-12

National Classification of Occupations (1 digit)	*Male*		*Female*	
	1983	*2011-12*	*1983*	*2011-12*
Professional, technical and related workers	3.7	5.7	2.4	6.5
Working proprietors, administrative, executive and managerial workers	1.7	8.1	0.5	3.7
Clerical and related workers	4.2	3.3	0.8	1.5
Sales workers	6.9	7.8	2.8	2.8
Service workers	3.9	3.7	4.0	5.7
Farmers, fishermen, hunters, loggers and related workers	60.3	41.5	78.7	58.2
Production and related workers, transport equipment operators and labourers	19.4	30.1	10.9	21.5
Total	100.0	100.0	100.0	100.0

Source: NSS (Mamgain, 2016).

A similar analysis of the composition of occupations across social groups (SC, ST, Muslims and others) shows clearly a concentration of SCs (scheduled castes) in unskilled labour, along with some other specific, generally low status or low skilled occupations—domestic service, mining, sweepers and cleaners, painters. There is a larger than average proportion of SCs in all of these occupations. Scheduled tribes (STs) have a somewhat similar profile, with a particularly high concentration among unskilled labourers. Muslims too have a distinctive occupational pattern. They are underrepresented in technical, professional and white collar occupations, but are more frequently found in small business, and in specific skilled or semi-skilled occupations such as tailoring, work in the food and tobacco industries, transport and some other manufacturing sub-sectors. These differences appear to be more persistent over time than those between women and men, for there is little change in the caste and community pattern over the period between 1983 and 2011-12.

This social distribution of occupations in part reflects a tendency for occupational opportunities to be transferred from one generation to the next. There is relatively little research on intergenerational mobility in India, but whatever there is tends to suggest that mobility is low. Motiram and Singh (2012) find that there is considerable persistence in occupations over generations, comparing sons with fathers, in both rural and urban areas. This is particularly strong at the bottom of the occupational hierarchy, and among SCs and STs. These groups are also most vulnerable to downward mobility, if fathers have relatively higher status occupations. Majumder's more detailed study (2010) found that upward mobility across generations is moderate for educational level but low for occupation. While the educational levels of the second generation are higher than those of their parents (in 2004), this is only imperfectly reflected in the occupational mobility matrix. People are stuck in their parental occupational class and whatever movement occurs is mostly among upper classes. Reddy and Swaminathan's study (2014) of 10 villages suggested that the main vehicle for intergenerational occupational mobility for people in rural India is migration to urban or semi-urban areas. Within the villages intergenerational occupational mobility was low, particularly among big farmers and manual workers. Scheduled Caste men who remained in the villages were unable to move out of rural manual employment.

7.2. Change Over Time

The second aspect of occupational inequality is change in occupational patterns over time. With economic growth and structural change, some occupations are expanding and others are contracting. Depending on the size and relative remuneration of each occupational category, inequality measured across the workforce as a whole may be increasing or decreasing. In India in recent years it has been professional, technical, administrative and managerial occupations that have been expanding fastest. These are the highest paid occupations, and while they only constitute only a small fraction of all employment, their share in the workforce rose from less than 5 per cent in 1983 to 13 per cent in 2011-12.

Table 7.2

Annual Growth Rates (%) of Number of Workers by Occupational Group

National Classification of Occupations (1 digit)	*Period*		
	1983 to 1993-94	*1993-94 to 2004-05*	*2004-05 to 2011-12*
Professional, technical and related workers	4.0	4.1	6.3
Working proprietors, administrative, executive and managerial workers	8.3	7.8	10.3
Clerical and related workers	3.9	1.3	1.4
Sales workers	4.6	3.8	-2.4
Service workers	1.8	4.3	0.2
Farmers, fishermen, hunters, loggers and related workers	1.9	0.8	-2.2
Production and related workers, transport equipment operators and labourers	3.7	4.0	4.7
Total	2.6	2.1	0.6

Source: NSS (Mamgain, 2016).

There has also been a substantial increase in the share of production, transport and related workers, especially of unskilled labourers. This is a much lower income category. To a large extent, this group's increased share corresponds to the decline in agricultural occupations. Altogether, these trends imply that outside agriculture, job growth has been concentrated in the highest and lowest paying occupations, widening wage inequality.

7.3. Occupational Wages

The third aspect of this issue is change in the relative wages and incomes of the occupations concerned. Figure 7.1 plots the ratio of the wages for 33 occupational categories to the overall mean wage in 2011-12 against the same ratio in 1993-94, for male, regular workers, using data from the NSS compiled by R.P. Mamgain.

Wage differentials are largely maintained over time, as can be seen from the close relationship between wage ratios in each period. Additionally, at the lower wage levels, the ratios are rather similar to 1993-94 in both 2004-05 and 2011-12—that is, the ratios are along or around the 45-degree line, perhaps averaging slightly below the line in 2004-05. However, at higher wage levels, most wage ratios are above the line. This tendency for the rise in the wage ratio to be correlated with the wage ratio in 1993-94 implies that wage differentials have increased. However there is not much difference in the pattern for 2004-05 and 2011-12, suggesting that most of the rise occurred before the former date.

Figure 7.1

Wage Ratio (Compared with the Mean) for Two Digit Occupations, 2004-05 and 2011-12 Graphed against 1993-94, Regular Male Workers

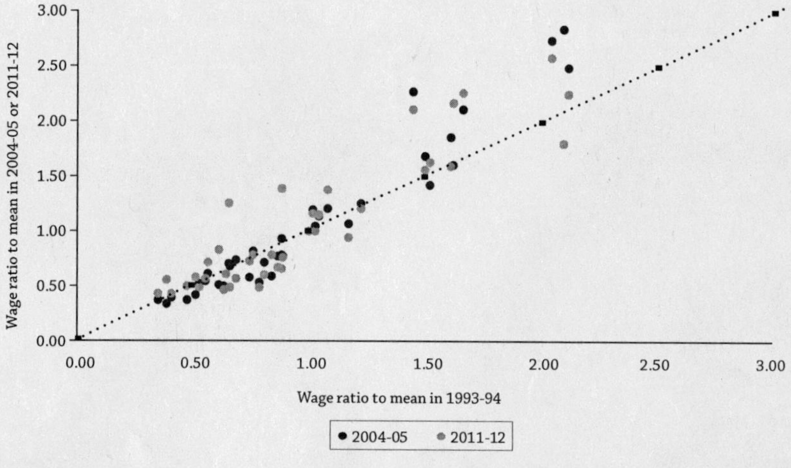

A similar pattern can be observed for female regular workers (Figure 7.2). The scatter is wider, and the sample is smaller because there are fewer women within the regular workforce. However, once again at the higher wage levels the tendency is for the wage ratio to rise, while at lower wage levels the tendency is for it to fall, so occupational wage inequality is widening.

While we also have data for casual workers, casual work is very small or atypical for the majority of occupations, so we cannot undertake the same analysis for this category. As was noted earlier, the ratio of casual to regular wages fell until 2004-05, but rose in the period up to 2011-12.

Figure 7.2

Wage Ratio (Compared with the Mean) for Two Digit Occupations, 2004-05 and 2011-12 Graphed against 1993-94, Regular Female Workers

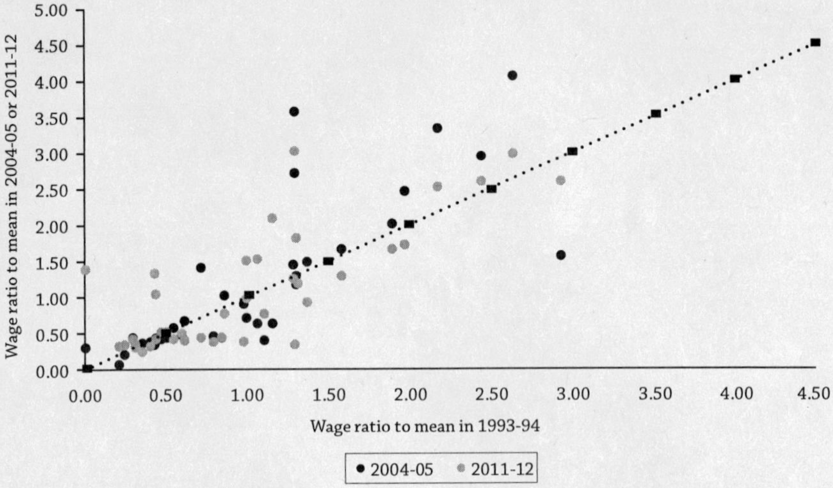

Overall, then, we can conclude that occupational factors did contribute to the widening of wage inequality in the last thirty years, both as a result of the rising share of higher wage occupations, and as a result of widening occupational wage differentials. This tendency towards growing inequality may have been partially offset by increased access for women to higher wage occupations, but the differences in opportunities among castes and communities do not show any similar tendency to decline.

8

Concluding Comments

This monograph provides some evidence on key dimensions of inequality in India and how they have changed over the last thirty years. We have looked at the overall degree and pattern of inequality in wages and in household expenditure, and at some of the key dimensions of this inequality, in terms of labour market structures, gender differentiation, differing opportunities across social and religious groups, returns to education and the regional pattern of growth and development.

The picture that emerges is complex. Inequalities take many forms and affect groups of the population in different ways. Nor are the relationships consistent in different parts of India, so what is observed at the national level may be an amalgam of different patterns in different regions.

When we look at different dimensions of inequality together, we find interactions which modify our understanding of the role of each dimension separately. The multi-level decompositions suggest, for instance, that caste and community differences are weakened when other factors such as education and occupation are taken into account, while gender differences persist. But this also implies a need to understand the indirect influence of caste and community through their impact on opportunity. All of these factors are intertwined, highlighting the need for caution in interpretation.

There is clearly a need for additional analysis of some major issues, in particular the contribution of regional differences and occupational patterns to inequality. A more complex model would be required to understand the role of education.

Finally, this work has been done in the context of a comparative study between India and Brazil. It is likely that this comparison will itself bring new perspectives which can inform the analysis in each country. So these results are best seen as an input to an as yet unfinished enterprise. But there are significant findings here, which can provide a platform for further empirical work.

References

Asadullah, M. Niaz and Gaston Yalonetzky (2012). "Inequality of Educational Opportunity in India: Changes Over Time and Across States". *World Development* 40(6): 1151-63, June.

Atkinson, A.B. (1983). *The Economics of Inequality.* London: Clarendon Press.

Barbosa, Alexandre de Freitas *et al.* (forthcoming). *Growth, Labour and Inequality in Brazil and India: A Comparative Study.* Sao Paulo: Cebrap and New Delhi: IHD.

Cacciamali, Maria Cristina, Gerry Rodgers, Vidya Soundararajan and Fabio Tatei (2015). "Wage Inequality in Brazil and India: A Quantitative Comparative Analysis", *Working Paper* 02/2015. New Delhi: Institute for Human Development.

Dev, S. Mahendra and C. Ravi (2007). "Poverty and Inequality: All-India and States, 1983-2005", *Economic and Political Weekly* 42(6): 509-21.

Dutta, V. Puja (2005). "Accounting for Wage Inequality in India", *PRUS Working Paper* no. 29. Poverty Research Unit, Department of Economics, University of Sussex. January. Available online at *https://www.sussex.ac.uk/webteam/gateway/file.php?name=wp29.pdf&site=260*, last accessed on 11 March 2015

Elbers, Chris, Peter Lanjouw, Johan Mistiaen, Berk Özler (2008). "Reinterpreting Between-Group Inequality", *Journal of Economic Inequality* 6:231-45.

Fields, Gary S. (2002). *Accounting for Income Inequality and its Change: A New Method, With Application to the Distribution of Earnings in the United States.* Cornell University ILR School. *http://digitalcommons.ilr.cornell.edu/articles/265/*

Ghose, Ajit K. (2014). "Globalisation, Growth and Employment in India", *Working Paper* 05/2014. New Delhi: Institute for Human Development.

Himanshu (2007). "Recent Trends in Poverty and Inequality: Some Preliminary Results", *Economic and Political Weekly,* 10 February.

India, National Sample Survey Organisation (various dates). *Unemployment and Employment Surveys, and Household Expenditure Surveys.* 38th Round (1983), 50th Round (1993-94), 61st Round (2004-05), 68th Round (2011-12). New Delhi, Ministry of Statistics and Plan Implementation.

Institute for Human Development (2014). *India: Labour and Employment Report.* New Delhi: Academic Foundation.

Jayadev, Arjun, Sripad Motiram and Vamsi Vakulabharanam (2007). "Patterns of Wealth Disparities in India During the Liberalisation Era", *Economic and Political Weekly* 42(38): 3853-63.

Krishna, Anirudh (2013). "Making it in India. Examining Social Mobility in Three Walks of Life", *Economic and Political Weekly*, 7 December.

Mahadevia, Darshini and Sandip Sarkar (2012). *Handbook of Urban Inequalities* New Delhi: Oxford University Press.

Majumder, Rajarshi (2010). "Intergenerational Mobility in Educational and Occupational Attainment: A Comparative Study of Social Classes in India", *Margin: The Journal of Applied Economic Research* 4(4): 463-94. Available at: *http://mpra.ub.uni-muenchen.de/40939/1/MPRA_paper_40939.pdf*

Mamgain, Rajendra P. (2016). "Occupational Diversification in India: Trends and Determinants", in K.P. Kannan, Rajendra P. Mamgain and Preet Rustagi (eds.), *Labour and Development: Essays in Honour of Professor T.S. Papola*. New Delhi: Academic Foundation. Forthcoming.

Mazumdar, D. (2010). "Decreasing Poverty and Increasing Inequality in India" in *Tackling Inequalities in Brazil, China, India and South Africa: The Role of Labour Market and Social Policies*. Paris: OECD. pp.157-207.

Mazumdar, Dipak and Sandip Sarkar (2008). *Globalization, Labor Markets and Inequality in India*. Abingdon, Oxon: Routledge.

Mazumdar, Dipak, Sandip Sarkar and Balwant Singh Mehta (2013). "Inequality in India". New Delhi: Institute for Human Development project Globalisation and Inequality (*mimeo*).

Motiram, Sripad and Ashish Singh (2012). "How Close Does the Apple Fall to the Tree? Some Evidence on Intergenerational Occupational Mobility from India", *WIDER Working Paper* 2012/101. Helsinki.

Motiram, Sripad and Vakulabharanam (2012). *Indian Inequality: Patterns and Changes, 1993-2010*. Available online at *http://www.igidr.ac.in/faculty/sripad/Sripad_Vamsi_IDR2012.pdf*, last accessed on 11 March 2015.

Nathan, Dev and Sandip Sarkar (2014). "Global Inequality, Rising Powers and Labour Standards", *Oxford Development Studies* 42(2): 278-95.

National Council of Applied Economic Research (2004-05). *India Human Development Survey*. *http://ihds.umd.edu*

Reddy, A. Bheemeshwar and Madhura Swaminathan (2014). "Intergenerational Occupational Mobility in Rural India: Evidence from Ten Villages", *Review of Agrarian Studies* 4(1). Available at: *http://ras.org.in/intergenerational_occupational_mobility_in_rural_india*

Sarkar, Sandip and Balwant Singh Mehta (2015). *Inequality and Employment in South Asia: Options for More Inclusive Economic Development*. Draft project report. New Delhi: Institute for Human Development.

Sarkar, Sandip and Balwant Singh Mehta (2010). "Income Inequality in India: Pre- and Post-Reform Periods", *Economic and Political Weekly* XLV(37), 11 September.

Sen, Amartya (1997). *On Economic Inequality*, New Delhi, Oxford.

Sen, Amartya and Himanshu (2004). "Poverty and Inequality in India 2: Widening Disparities during the 1990s", *Economic and Political Weekly*, 25 September.

Shorrocks, A.F. (1980). "The Class of Additively Decomposable Inequality Measures", *Econometrica* 48: 613-25.

Singh, Ashish, Upasak Das and Tushar Agarwal (2013). "How Inclusive has Regular Employment been in India? A Dynamic View", *The European Journal of Development Research* 25: 486-94.

Singh, Ashish, Abhishek Singh, Saseendran Pallikadavath and Faujdar Ram (2014). "Gender Differentials in Inequality of Educational Opportunities: New Evidence from an Indian Youth Study", *European Journal of Development Research* 26: 707-24.

Vakulabharanam, V. (2010). "Does Class Matter? Class Structure and Worsening Inequality in India", *Economic and Political Weekly* 45(29): 67-76.

Weisskopf, T. (2011). "Why Worry About Inequality in the Booming Indian Economy", *Economic and Political Weekly* 46(47): 41-51.